THE BREAKFAST BOOK

The Breakfast Book

Andrew Dalby

REAKTION BOOKS

Published by
Reaktion Books Ltd
33 Great Sutton Street
London EC1V 0DX, UK
www.reaktionbooks.co.uk

First published 2013

Printed and bound in China

British Library Cataloguing in Publication Data

Dalby, Andrew, 1947–
The breakfast book.
1. Breakfasts.
2. Breakfasts—History.
I. Title
394.1'252-dc23
ISBN 978 1 78023 086 3

CONTENTS

Foreword

I knew at the age of twelve that I would write a breakfast book one day, after reading in Isaac Asimov's *Inside the Atom* (1956: probably remaindered, like all the other books Uncle Jim gave me as Christmas presents) the claim that scientists would soon split atoms as commonly 'as you and I eat potatoes for breakfast'. How strange that Asimov should believe his average reader would eat potatoes for breakfast! I had to sort that matter out sooner or later.

I claim that there is as yet not a single general history of breakfast in existence, global or otherwise, and I can name at least one reason for this. When attempting to write histories of human habits, such as meals and mealtimes, the honest historian will remember and repeat Arnold Palmer's warning (in *Movable Feasts*, 1952): 'Hardly anything in this book is quite, quite true.' Glance at the discoveries of which I am proudest: are they quite, quite true? For example, the surprising parallels among the four breakfasts, spanning 32 centuries, that are narrated in the prologue; the tragedy of Damer's muffins, told in the epilogue; the estimate in chapter Five that *Ulysses* offers the second longest exploration in literature of the consciousness of a single would-be breakfaster; and the claim in the same chapter to have identified the longest of all such explorations . . .

This is both less and more than a global history: there are indeed several histories here. The anthropological and linguistic origins of breakfast are told in chapter One; a chronological history focusing on Europe (the only continent, I believe, for which anything resembling such a story can be fully told) is presented in chapter Two, a geographical history in chapter Three; the social and psychological constraints on breakfast are teased out in chapters Four and Five. The images, complementing the text, help to show what people have seen, or wanted to see, as they breakfast. There are even statistics, but statistics tell us little, and breakfast statistics less than most. What people do, and what they think they do, are questions more revealingly answered when they write fiction and autobiography. The history that I offer here grows out of what people have said about breakfast, what they have meant and what they have thought.

Prologue:
Four Breakfasts

The world's first literary breakfast took place in a mountain hut on the Greek island of Ithaca in the year 1174 BC. Ten years after Troy fell to the Greek army, Odysseus has arrived home, incognito, after his long wanderings.

> The two of them, Odysseus and Eumaios, were preparing breakfast in the hut as the sun rose, after stirring up the fire and sending the herdsmen out with the pigs to pasture . . . Suddenly Odysseus turned to the noble swineherd and spoke winged words: 'Eumaios, some friend of yours or someone familiar is on his way to us – because I hear footsteps, and your dogs are not barking but fawning.'
>
> He had not even finished speaking when his own dear son stood in the doorway. Startled, Eumaios jumped up. The bowls that he was working with, mixing fiery wine, fell out of his hands . . .
>
> Odysseus went and sat down again, and the swineherd made a pile of green brushwood, with fleeces on it; there Odysseus' dear son sat down. The swineherd put before them platters of roast meat that had been left uneaten the day before, and quickly piled bread alongside in baskets, and poured honey-sweet wine into a mug. He himself sat down opposite godly Odysseus, and they set their hands to the food that was ready.

Rembrandt, *Belshazzar's Feast*, *c.* 1636–8, oil on canvas. A supper, but it captures the surprise that is typical of breakfast.

If poets told the truth, and if the traditional chronology of the Trojan War had anything to do with reality, this breakfast would be a verifiable, datable fact and *The Breakfast Book* would start here.

Things are not so simple. As the nine Muses once admitted to Homer's rival Hesiod, 'We know how to tell many lies that seem to be true.' The Muses inspire poets, and for that reason poets, too, tell many lies. Now we know that the *Odyssey*, in which this breakfast is narrated, was written down several hundred years after the Trojan War, at whatever date archaeologists eventually agree to place that war, if indeed they all one day agree that it took place. Modern researchers on oral epics, concurring with Hesiod and the Muses, doubt whether even the most crucial historical details are reliably transmitted by poets over such a long period. Those crucial details would include the homeland of Odysseus, his date, the reality of his wanderings and his precise connection with the Trojan War, if he had any connection with it at all. We must finally accept not just that there is doubt whether this breakfast happened, but that the probabilities are against it.

So let's take a second literary breakfast, dated 1,200 years after the one on Ithaca and located on the shore of the Sea of Tiberias, 1,000 miles to the southeast.

> There together were Simon Peter, Thomas called the Twin, Nathanael from Cana in Galilee, the sons of Zebedaios, and two of the other disciples. Simon Peter says to them, 'I'm going fishing.' They say to him, 'We're coming with you.'

Duccio di Buoninsegna, *Christ Appears to His Disciples at the Sea of Tiberias* (from the Maestà altar, Siena), 1311. This, one of the oldest evocations of the incident, shows the miraculous catch.

They went out and got into their boat, and they caught nothing all night. When dawn came Jesus was standing on the shore, but the disciples didn't know that it was Jesus. So Jesus says to them, 'Haven't you got any relish, boys?' They say to him, 'No.'

He said to them, 'Drop your net on the right side of the ship and you'll find something.' They did so, and now they couldn't pull it up for the quantity of fish. And the disciple Jesus loved says to Peter, 'It's the master.'

When Simon Peter heard that it was the master he pulled his cloak around himself, because he had nothing on, and dived into the sea. The other disciples came to land in their boat (they were not far out, about two hundred cubits) dragging the net with the fish in it. When they jumped out on shore, they see embers laid, and a fish set over it, and bread. Jesus says to them, 'Fetch some of the fish you've caught.'

Simon Peter came up and pulled the net to shore, laden with a hundred and fifty-three big fish. Even though there were so many the net wasn't split. Jesus says to them, 'Come and have breakfast.'

None of the disciples cared to ask him, 'Who are you?' They knew it was the master. Jesus goes and gets the bread and gives it out to them, and the fish as well.

This was the third time that Jesus appeared to his disciples after waking from the dead.

The lines that follow this story tell us that the disciple Jesus loved was the reporter of the incident and was also the writer of the Gospel. Some accept this as literally true; many do not. If we accept it, we are accepting this narrative as an eyewitness report, and therefore as very strong evidence that the breakfast really took place on the shore of the Sea of Tiberias in the year of the Crucifixion (around AD 35). As to who the visitor was, the reader still has to decide.

Now a third literary breakfast. The setting is Fressingfield in Suffolk, well over 1,000 miles northwest of Ithaca; we are once more leaping ahead 1,200 years or thereabouts; and our source is the popular play

Friar Bacon and Friar Bungay. Lord Lacy and his friends Ermsby and Warren have ridden through the night. Lacy is about to redeem his promise to marry the keeper's daughter. Will she take him?

> LACY: Come on, my wags, we're near the Keeper's lodge.
> Here have I oft walked in the watery meads
> And chatted with my lovely Margaret . . .
> ERMSBY: Choose you, fair damsel: yet the choice is yours:
> Either a solemn nunnery or the court,
> God or Lord Lacy: which contents you best? . . .
> MARGARET: The flesh is frail. My lord doth know it well,
> That when he comes with his enchanting face,
> Whate'er betide, I cannot say him nay . . .
> ERMSBY: I pray thee, my Lord of Sussex, why art thou in a
> brown study?
> WARREN: To see the nature of women, that, be they never
> so near God, yet they love to die in a man's arms.
> LACY: What have you fit for breakfast? We have hied
> And posted all this night to Fressingfield.
> MARGARET: Butter and cheese, and umbles of a deer,
> Such as poor keepers have within their lodge.
> LACY : And not a bottle of wine?
> MARGARET: We'll find one for my lord.
> LACY : Come, Sussex, let us in – we shall have more,
> For she speaks least, to hold her promise sure.

This incident did not happen. Robert Greene, who wrote *Friar Bacon and Friar Bungay* in 1590 or thereabouts, knew very little about his subjects – very little, in particular, about Henry de Lacy, Earl of Lincoln and protector of England at the time of Edward I. It was true that Lacy courted a Margaret, but that's almost the only accurate fact in Greene's play, and it's a coincidence. The historical Margaret was a noblewoman, not a keeper's daughter, and she didn't live in Suffolk: there can have been no morning encounter at Fressingfield and no breakfast.

Not one of these descriptions of breakfasts can be accepted as straight history. In truth, very few can. In social history it doesn't necessarily matter. Breakfasts are not minuted, and yet the best breakfasts – the ones that are most worth recalling – are remembered or recreated in the memory.

Some Questions

Let's admit the concept of a main daily meal. It may be taken at midday, in the early or late afternoon, in the early or late evening: evidence will be found in different cultures for all those times, and many people will be found who take two meals of this kind. But the big meal of the day will not normally be taken between dawn and late morning. Let's admit, then, the concept of a lesser meal, preceding other meals, taken some time in the morning, and let's allow it to consist of anything between a quick drink and a substantial collation. Let's call it breakfast.

Questions begin to crystallize.

First, if we are right to generalize that breakfast is always different from other meals – and that the big meal is never normally taken in the morning – why is it so? Does the size and solidity of breakfast differ from one culture to another? Does it differ according to age, according to daily activities, according to wealth and status?

Next, exploring how fundamental is the distinction between breakfast and other meals, do people choose breakfast foods differently? A different range of foods? A smaller range? If foods chosen at other meals vary from day to day, do foods chosen for breakfast vary similarly – and, if they don't, why are we conservative at breakfast?

Taking a historical perspective – this is a history – have breakfasts always existed? Has the daily timetable of meals changed over time? Have fashions in the size and contents of breakfast changed? Are these things changing more rapidly now than they have in the past? If it was ever valid to generalize for every human, or for each culture, about meal habits – as I did above – is it equally valid to do this today, or has people's behaviour become less rule-bound than it used to be?

Lastly, do people behave differently about breakfast? Do we serve it differently, eat it differently or in a different place, talk differently or not at all at breakfast? Do people think differently about breakfast,

Frederic S. Remington, *A Cavalryman's Breakfast on the Plains*, *c.* 1892, oil on canvas.

before, during, after? Accepting, as the odd anthropologist quite possibly does, that meals have a meaning, does breakfast have a meaning?

Some Answers

Each of the three breakfast narratives above offers food for thought (to coin a phrase). But take the three together. Not only do they pose for us the kind of questions, as sketched above, that a social history of breakfast needs to explore, but they also suggest some possible answers to those questions, particularly the last ones. Breakfast does perhaps differ in some essential quality from other meals. These three breakfast narratives certainly have common features that they do not share with narratives of dinners from similar times and places.

First, they were unplanned. Yes, no doubt Eumaios and his pig-men ate something every morning, around dawn, after the pigs had been driven out to their 'pasture', but this breakfast was different: it was partly got ready by an anonymous wanderer who had been allowed to stay overnight. Yes, no doubt Peter and his comrades usually hoped to eat something when they returned to land after a night's fishing, but this breakfast was different: it was prepared by a stranger on the shore who had already lit the fire and was providing the bread. All they had to do was to supply the fish. Yes, no doubt Margaret's father, the keeper in *Friar Bacon and Friar Bungay*, wanted breakfast when he came in after early work in field or forest, but this breakfast was different: unexpected but welcome guests who had ridden through the night were demanding food.

Admittedly there are special features in each of these three narratives that need to be put to one side if we hope to make general use of the stories. The beggar was Odysseus, Eumaios' old master, in disguise. It doesn't matter: he maintains his disguise, and we may imagine that the breakfast would have happened in just the same way whoever he was. The stranger on the shore was Jesus, not long after his resurrection, and the fact that after finding no fish all night the fishermen made a plentiful catch just in time for breakfast was one of his miracles. It doesn't matter: whoever the stranger was, he had the bread and they, if they were lucky, would have had some fish to serve as relish and to help the bread to go down. Lacy's eventful courtship of the keeper's daughter included a rivalry with Prince Edward, the future Edward I, before the prince submitted to his dynastic destiny and married Eleanor of Castile. It doesn't matter: we are allowed to conclude that any respectable guest, royal or not so royal, would have been welcome to invite themselves to breakfast at the keeper's lodge.

Second, the three breakfast menus differ strikingly from dinner menus of the same times and places, some of which are available for comparison. Eumaios serves Odysseus and Telemachos with 'platters of roast meat that had been left uneaten the day before'; alongside the meat he sets out bread in baskets, and honey-sweet wine in a mug – plenty of baskets but only one mug. I need hardly point out how this differs from the meal that Eumaios had served the previous evening. The bread and wine are of course always present, the basis of every ancient Greek meal large or small, but the difference is in the relish. Conceptually there is all the difference in the world between

Claude Monet, *Le Déjeuner: panneau decorative, c.* 1874, oil on canvas.

meat that's roasted for the occasion (which is the typical centrepiece of a good literary dinner at almost any time and place from Homeric Greece to the present day) and meat that had been left uneaten the day before. Margaret offers Lacy and his saddle-sore companions umbles of a deer – venison offal. There is no room to specify in Robert Greene's blank verse whether this takes the form of umble pie or some charcuterie-like preparation. Alongside the offal there is butter and cheese. These in themselves demand the presence of bread; bread, butter and cheese are to be imagined as always present, the basis of every meal. Again, there's no need to ask how this differs from the dinner that would have been prepared for such guests at the keeper's lodge. Any literary dinner worth the name would have included fresh meat and almost certainly roast venison. And at any self-respecting dinner there would have been no need for Lacy to ask, 'And not a bottle of wine?' Yet he is in medieval England, a country in which wine doesn't grow on trees and wine is not the obvious breakfast beverage. To keep her promise – 'We'll find one for my lord' – Margaret might well have had to borrow a bottle from the neighbours.

Two breakfasts, then, at which the relish is a properly frugal side-effect or by-product of previous dinners. Breakfast on the shore of the Sea of Tiberias is quite different from these. There is, as always, bread. For relish there may be nothing at all, but the assumption – demonstrated by the stranger's initial and unremarkable question, 'Haven't you got any relish, boys?' as demanded of a boatload of fishermen on their way back to land – is that if there is any relish it will be newly caught fish. Now in the case of these fishermen their dinner, too, might well have been bread and fish or bread and nothing at all. Yet there is still a difference, though this time the narrative doesn't help us much in identifying it. Breakfast will provide the smallest fish, quick to fry or grill, least profitable to sell; dinner will be fish soup made with the fish that didn't sell, accompanied by the vegetables and herbs that no one had time to gather for breakfast. As far as flavour is concerned, breakfast may well turn out to be the best meal of the day.

And so on the basis of these three breakfasts we have already begun to consider some of the big questions. Do people choose breakfast foods differently? Yes, they choose some of the same foods but they choose them differently. Do people think differently about breakfast? Yes, it appears that they do. Breakfasts are impromptu and not planned in every detail. There's often no time; and things happen; and, when it comes to breakfasts, the more unforeseen they are, the better; or the more unforeseen, the more they are worth remembering. Let me now reinforce these impressions by taking a fourth literary breakfast, written seventy years ago by John Steinbeck in *The Grapes of Wrath* (1939). It's a long scene – the longest meal in the novel – but it requires only brief quotation.

Tom Joad, on parole, returns home to rural Oklahoma to find his parents and the whole family about to set out eastwards to find a living in California. He and his travelling companion, the former preacher Casy, arrive at sunrise. Pa, who is out in the yard working on the

Family of Harry Fain, coal loader, at breakfast, Kentucky, 1946.

truck, is the first to see him. 'S'pose I go in an' say: "Here's some fellas want some breakfast,"' Pa muses, wondering how best to surprise Ma with the news of Tom's return. 'She'll yell breakfast in a minute. I heard her slap the salt pork in the pan a good time ago.' Here's another unforeseen breakfast: Ma doesn't yet know that there will be two new faces, one of whom is her son. The family has very little money, but – like the keeper's household at Fressingfield – enough resources to offer hospitality. 'Let 'em come,' says Ma, still not knowing who they are. '"We got a'plenty. Tell 'em they got to wash their han's. The bread is done. I'm jus' takin' up the side-meat now." And the sizzle of the angry grease came from the stove.' There is play with regional vocabulary here: Pa's salt pork is Ma's side-meat and some of us might have called it bacon. In other words, there is again the usual choice of bread and relish for breakfast, a relish that is meaty indeed, closely related to the pork that might be the centrepiece of an ideal dinner, but distinguished from it.

> She was lifting the curling slices of pork from the frying-pan. The oven door was open, and a great pan of high brown biscuits stood waiting there . . . 'Come in,' she said. 'Jus' lucky I made plenty bread this morning.' . . . She shook flour into the deep grease to make gravy, and her hand was white with flour'

Biscuits? Here is regional vocabulary once more. Ma's bread is the narrator's biscuit, and I am on Ma's side here: it becomes clear that these are the kind of biscuits that soak up gravy, and I have never known biscuits do that. For more help with this see the Recipes section.

One of the not fully planned features of this breakfast is that not everyone can sit around the table or even find a place to perch in the kitchen. 'Ma waved the flies away from the bowl of gravy. "We ain't got room to set down," she said.' Casy is prevailed upon to say grace. '"A-men", said Granma, and she fell to her breakfast, and broke down the soggy biscuits with her hard old toothless gums . . . There was no talk until the food was gone, the coffee drunk.' Here, now, is one of the few substantive differences between this and the older breakfasts quoted earlier. Throughout that long period, from 1200 BC to AD 1200 and later, human beings managed to breakfast without the stimulating drinks – *thé, café, chocolat* – that we now take for granted.

The four breakfasts quoted above have one more common feature. It is one that they do not share with – to take an example close at hand – my usual breakfast. They all take place around dawn, and yet those who are going to eat them have already been working (Eumaios' herdsmen, the fishermen on the Sea of Tiberias and Pa Joad) or travelling (Telemachos, Lacy and his companions, Tom Joad and Casy) or, if nothing else, at least preparing breakfast for all the rest (Eumaios and Odysseus, the stranger on the shore, Ma Joad). The exceptions are interesting: they are Granma and Grampa Joad, who are too old to be expected to do any reliable work and, possibly, Margaret the keeper's daughter. We don't know what Margaret has been doing, but she is

Henri de Toulouse-Lautrec, *The Artist's Mother, Comtesse Adèle-Zoé de Toulouse-Lautrec, at Breakfast, Malromé Chateau*, 1883, oil on canvas.

certainly up, dressed and out, and will no doubt soon be preparing breakfast for her father and his unexpected guests.

Most of us in the twenty-first century do very little before breakfast (unless we are travelling, in which case we are still quite likely to set out early and eat breakfast on the way). Before breakfasting at home we may do nothing more than crawl out of bed, wash, dress and open the fridge door. On this initial evidence the breakfast that we take represents something of an innovation.

Student volunteers eating breakfast at a FEMA base camp after Hurricane Katrina, New Orleans, 2006.

one

Breakfast:
Origin, Evolution
and Name

The greatest single innovation in the history of human food was the Neolithic revolution – which was a more gradual process than the word 'revolution' suggests. Before humans took up the three revolutionary habits of keeping animals, planting crops and storing the resulting produce, they never knew where their next meal was coming from. It might be the result of luck when hunting; it might be the result of wayside finds among herbs, fruits, flowers, grubs and insects. It would very probably be a combination of both, the hunted meat provided and cooked by the men, the foraged food found by the children and women and cooked by the latter.

The new habits that constituted this revolution and marked the beginning of the Neolithic period or New Stone Age came into being at different dates in various parts of the world. In some places they were never adopted and the hunter-gatherer lifestyle typical of the Palaeolithic period or Old Stone Age persisted. Even where the Neolithic revolution took effect, it didn't necessarily happen all at once. You might store produce without planting it: bees and squirrels do, so why not humans? You might begin to keep animals for meat before it occurs to you that you can dry or salt the meat and in this way make it last. You would not, however, plant crops on a large scale without having some means of storing the produce: since nearly all staple crops are seasonal, by failing to store what you can't immediately eat you would waste nearly all your effort. Having thus learned to store grain, you might then eventually notice that effort in stock-keeping is saved if you kill the animals when they are fully grown but still young, thus offering in the greatest quantity the meat that is most easily cooked and digested; and since animals reproduce on a seasonal cycle you can only follow this method without significant waste once you have learned to preserve and store the meat.

When you know how to store meat and flour, there you have your bacon and bread for every day's breakfast. You can rely on it. It will revive you after your early morning work and nourish you for your day's labour in the fields – until, one year, the harvest fails or the stored meat and flour is somehow lost or enemies drive you off your land. Then the system collapses and starvation threatens. There is a direct line from the beginning of the Neolithic period to *The Grapes of Wrath*.

Before Breakfast

As a hypothesis we will propose a complete absence of breakfast before the Neolithic revolution.

There are not many discussions of this point by anthropologists. This can hardly mean that we are ahead of them and that they have not yet thought to pose the question of breakfast, so it must mean that they think it too obvious and trivial for serious enquiry. When anthropologists notice that a community under observation has a habit of taking breakfast, they describe the habit, as we shall soon see: the time of day, the foods usually taken, whether there are differences among men, women and children. But in the case of hunter-gatherer communities, who live in a way that is closer than any other now observable to the human communities during the Palaeolithic period, anthropologists in general don't describe any breakfasts. Therefore, since anthropologists are observant, sensitive and healthy people who fancy a morning croissant and cup of hot chocolate as much as anyone, we are forced to assume that in hunter-gatherer communities there are no breakfasts for the anthropologists to share.

At first I hoped that Claude Lévi-Strauss would have helped at this point. He gathered the largest body of data ever compiled on patterns of thought (particularly patterns of thought about food) in a vast region – the Amazon basin – in which many peoples lived as hunter-gatherers. Mealtimes are a pattern of behaviour that is surely reflected in patterns of thought. And yet, unfortunately, in the four volumes of Lévi-Strauss' *Mythologiques* the question of mealtimes – not where or how or what one eats, but when in the day and how frequently – seldom arises. Unless I'm mistaken the phrase *petit déjeuner* (the unambiguous term for 'breakfast' in Lévi-Strauss' French) does not occur even once. The word *déjeuner* itself (which in twentieth-century French equates to 'lunch') is difficult to find. This again, I take it, does not mean that Lévi-Strauss' primary sources didn't notice breakfast or lunch when it occurred, nor that they weren't interested in either meal. It means that in these hunter-gatherer communities there was no breakfast.

The reason is clear, and it also explains the absence of reference to lunch. In modern hunter-gatherer communities, as in those communities of the distant prehistoric past that were as yet untouched by the Neolithic revolution, the business of agricultural production and consequent seasonal surpluses did not exist. There was in general no system of food storage. The greater part of each day was spent gathering or hunting for food. When that task reached its natural end, the next task of the day was to prepare and eat the food that had been gathered. The natural end of the food-collecting task came, in cooler seasons, towards the end of the day when the light began to fail: we have, therefore, no difficulty in giving the name 'dinner' to the meal that eventually followed. In hot seasons, if it made no sense to go on with the food-collecting business all day, the task came to its natural end around noon when the heat reached its peak, and the food would be prepared and eaten, in a more leisurely way, in the afternoon. But it would hardly be appropriate to call it 'lunch': it remained the one major – and probably the only – meal of the day.

Adult humans can easily accustom themselves to a one-main-meal-a-day pattern, and many do. The classical Greek author of the essay *Ancient Medicine* was aware of two daily timetables, both widespread in his time (we are in the late fifth century BC, incidentally, and this author may have been the famous Hippokrates or may not):

> Eating once a day suits some healthy people, and they have made this their rule; others, because it suits them, take lunch. There are some again who adopt one rule or the other for

pleasure or some similar incidental cause. It does not matter to most people which rule they adopt, eating once a day or taking lunch; there are some, though, who are really affected when they vary their usual habit, even for a single day or less, and suffer severe discomfort. If they take lunch although it does not suit them they soon become heavy and sluggish in body and mind, beset with yawning, sleepiness and thirst; if they then go on to take dinner they get wind, colic and diarrhoea. In many people, even if they merely divide between two meals the same quantity of food that they have learned to absorb once a day, such a change can initiate serious illness.

The one-meal-a-day pattern which (I have argued) was the normal one before the Neolithic revolution, and which was common enough in Hippokrates' time, is less common in ours. Most of us expect lunch; many of us breakfast too.

From Bacon to Cheese

The Neolithic revolution began about nine thousand years ago in the Near East, spread outwards towards Greece and Iran and onwards both east and west. It brought agriculture, food storage and breakfast.

The reason, as is now clear (and can be seen from all four literary breakfasts of chapter One), is that breakfast demands stored food. At the time of day when breakfast is taken no one in the average household

Lute Pease, *Adventures of Powder Pete: Flapjacks for Breakfast*, 1926, cartoon. Flapjacks are pancakes, as they often are in American English.

has time for full-scale cooking. Frying bacon and other kinds of cooked meat and offal is quite practicable. Making a porridge from stored meal is good. Toasting or frying already-baked bread is fine. Grilling small fish, the idea that occurred to the stranger on the shore and was taken up by the disciples from the boat, is of course perfect. Eating freshly baked bread, if someone woke up in the night to start it baking (and probably to feed the baby at the same time) is heavenly. Refrying cooked meat, if this is what Eumaios and Odysseus were doing, is quite all right too; or the cooked meat, kept overnight, can be eaten cold. No problem. These breakfast ideas demand no more than a few minutes' labour in the morning.

None of this works if there is no flour to make the bread in the first place. It does not work if there is no salted or dried meat. It does not work if, as was the custom among hunter-gatherers, all the freshly roasted meat was eaten up the night before. Breakfast became feasible at the Neolithic revolution and not before.

The menu was as yet limited. The general view among archaeologists (not all subscribe to it, admittedly) is that early in the Neolithic age animals were kept for their meat alone. The idea of using their milk did not at first occur to anyone. If these theorists have it right, the Neolithic revolution was followed, about three thousand years later, by a 'secondary products revolution' that brought the use of wool and milk. The distinguishing feature of these products is that the animal goes on producing them and does not have to be killed to get them. But milk requires special treatment if it is to be put to full and economical use. In pre-modern conditions it will not keep fresh for more than a few hours and it will not travel at all. Even butter was of very limited use before the coming of refrigeration: it takes considerable labour to make it, and trouble must be taken over its storage if it is not to go to waste. The real revolution came when it was discovered how to conserve the rich nutritional value of milk by turning it into cheese. Cheese, well made and well stored, will keep for weeks, months or even years.

Cheese was well known to the ancient Egyptians, to the Sumerians and those who followed them in Mesopotamia, to the Hittites and the prehistoric Greeks. It was familiar to the poet who composed the *Odyssey*: we know this because the monstrous Cyclops, from whom

Floris Gerritsz. van Schooten, *Breakfast*, 17th century, oil on wood.

Odysseus barely escapes, is not only a man-eater but a cheesemaker. So it is the merest chance, perhaps, that no cheese is offered for breakfast at Eumaios' farm: he is of course a pig-keeper, not a goatherd, but the goatherd Melanthios is a part of the same economic unit, which therefore certainly produced cheese. Now if we believe (as some always did, and some classicists probably still do) that the lifestyle described in the *Odyssey* is perfect and logical and a distinct improvement on our own, the absence of cheese at Eumaios' breakfast can have nothing to do with chance: it must be evidence of rational thought, and probably of well-calculated economy. Yesterday Eumaios generously killed a sucking pig to provide dinner for his unexpected guest, the beggar – Odysseus in disguise. There is some meat left over, and in the Homeric world it will not be wasted, ergo they must eat it at breakfast. Setting aside theories about the Homeric world, we need to keep this example in mind. We will find many further cases in which breakfast consists of leftovers from the previous day.

There being no cheese at Eumaios' breakfast, nothing but bread and fish on the shore of the Sea of Tiberias and no milk or cheese produced on the farm that the Joads are being forced to abandon, cheese is on offer at only one of the four breakfasts quoted in chapter One – the breakfast at which Margaret, the keeper's daughter, proposes butter and cheese alongside the 'umbles of a deer'.

Sources for a History of Breakfast

The Neolithic revolution is one of the landmarks of archaeology, and it has supplied a hypothetical starting point for our enquiry. If we accept the secondary products revolution as a reality, it gives a second and firmer landmark: from that point onwards additional stored foods became available and were potential ingredients for breakfast.

Archaeology will tell us this much about the history of breakfast but it will tell us practically nothing more. The reason is obvious. Foods leave rich archaeological evidence: the bones discarded when meat is prepared or eaten; the seeds used in cooking and spicing; the containers in which foods and drinks are made and stored and transported and prepared; crockery and cutlery; and, aside from all that, botanical and agricultural remains. For many eras and places it's possible to develop a detailed list of foods that people ate. Often we can say fairly accurately when a new food was introduced. Occasionally we can even distinguish what was eaten by the rich and privileged from what was left to the poor and deprived. Bones from human burial may additionally show signs of malnutrition and starvation – further evidence of food and the lack of it.

But none of this has much to do with patterns of daily eating. As *Ancient Medicine* correctly tells us, people may take meals once or twice a day or more often, eating the same total amount but at different intervals. Just as some take lunch and some don't, some take breakfast and some don't. Archaeology can practically never tell us anything about this. We may guess that the foods taken at breakfast and those taken at dinner are different; archaeologists may find evidence of those foods, but they can't confirm that some were eaten in the morning and others in the evening. As far as archaeological evidence is concerned our guess will never (I think) be anything more than a guess.

This is why the history of breakfast has to be written from four sources, and very largely from these alone.

One source is the contemporary written record. I say 'contemporary' on purpose because it is necessary to emphasize that literature can only serve usefully for the social history of the period in which it was written. Look back one more time at the four breakfasts quoted in the prologue. There, as almost-timeless models of possible breakfasts, they served their purpose. It was amusing to notice that three of them happened to be set at 1,200-year intervals. But as specimens in a social history of breakfast they have to be re-categorized.

Two of them were (let me now admit it openly) historical fiction.

Friar Bacon and Friar Bungay, with the story of Lacy and his love for Margaret, was written in about 1590. Its ambition was to amuse Elizabethan and (as it would turn out) Jacobean audiences in London theatres, and over the next forty years it succeeded in this ambition. Those audiences enjoyed historical plays, both tragic and light-hearted, but knew little and cared less about social history. Dramatists like Robert Greene sometimes knew slightly more, but they also knew better than to turn a play into a lecture. Meals presented and described in Elizabethan historical plays are Elizabethan meals with, at the most, occasional details that would give an audience the impression of being historical. Hence breakfast at the keeper's lodge is breakfast in 1590, fictionalized and adapted to the Elizabethan stage; it is not breakfast in 1250.

The position is the same with the story of Odysseus' return to Ithaca. The purpose of the *Odyssey* was to give pleasure to audiences of heroic tales in the seventh century BC. It succeeded, of course, and continued to give pleasure for much longer than its author can have foreseen. The early audiences, and the poets who gave them pleasure, knew nothing at all about social history. The only record that could have supplied information about social history was the oral poetic tradition and this, though apparently immutable, was in truth ever-changing. Meals in early Greek epic are seventh-century BC meals, fictionalized, described in the traditional language of a living oral tradition; they are not meals in the time of the heroes of the twelfth century BC.

The other two breakfasts were contemporary. John Steinbeck was writing about his own time. He knew how it was both in California and in Oklahoma; his aim was to convince his readers that it was this way and that it needed to change. The author of John's Gospel, whether the disciple whom Jesus loved or not and whether or not truly a participant in the breakfast on the shore, wrote not many years after the events described and had every reason to make the incidental details seem realistic; his aim was to convince audiences that this stuff happened. These two quotations raise the issue of whether, in a social history of breakfast, descriptions of breakfasts that really happened – actual historical events – deserve greater respect than fictional breakfasts. They raise it and they go a long way to show why, to a social historian, the difference need not matter very much. We don't know whether to take the breakfast on the shore as uncomplicated fact, and we don't know whether Steinbeck participated in a breakfast in Oklahoma that was anything like the breakfast he described. We only know that these authors wanted to be read and taken seriously. And that's exactly where we are with the authors of memoirs, biographies and histories when they happen to describe a breakfast that really happened: they are still writing for an audience, they aren't under oath, their purpose is to be read and taken seriously. Their distance from reality may be exactly the same as that of John Steinbeck and John the Evangelist, or a little more, or a little less. It depends how they balance their memories and the space at their disposal against their overall aim to be read.

The most apparently gritty and businesslike of historical breakfasts are those found in the successive *Household Ordinances* laid down for the English royal family. 'The Queen's Breakfast per annum, by estimacion, £70. 0s. 0d.' is one example in the 'Elmham Ordinance', a set of regulations laid out in meticulous detail in 1526 in Thomas Wolsey's office during the short period when he ruled the royal household. This is all very fine, but we can get no truth from it except a fair certainty that the queen's private household (the queen was Catherine of Aragon at this point) was to be supplied with breakfast. How much of it, if any, did she eat? How many shared it? How much was really spent on it? Seventy pounds a year is Wolsey's target, but the Elmham Ordinance, like some others in the series, expatiates boringly on how targets for savings have never in the past been met. We may doubt whether Wolsey's targets were met either.

Jean Leon Gerome Ferris, *The Birth of Pennsylvania*, c. 1910. William Penn at Charles
II's breakfast table in the year 1680.

Among the tastiest and most varied of historical breakfasts are
those in Samuel Pepys's diaries. As a sample, here is Pepys's record,
under the date of 25 May 1660, of the last meal on shipboard taken by
Charles II and his two brothers James, Duke of York, and Henry, Duke
of Gloucester, before they disembarked at Dover on their triumphant
return from nine years of exile.

By the morning we were come close to the land and everybody
made ready to get on shore. The King and the two Dukes did
eat their breakfast before they went, and there being set some
Shipps diet before them, only to show them the manner of the
Shipps diet: they eat of nothing else but pease and pork and
boiled beef. I spoke with the Duke of York upon business, who
called me Pepys by name,

he remarks proudly. Pepys was always anxious to be noticed, and never more so than at this moment when the entourage of royalty in exile was jostling for position in a future administration.

Now this, from Pepys, is real history. We know the menu, we know the three breakfasters, we know exactly what they ate (washed down with wine? Almost certainly, but that isn't on record). We know where they were – we can almost hear the water lapping and the creaking of the beams. But this breakfast is a sport of circumstance. The royal dukes didn't get 'pease and pork and boiled beef' at every day's breakfast. Every other day they had whatever the captain had carefully provided for his royal passengers, and Pepys doesn't tell us what that was. Today they had demanded to know what the regular 'shipps diet' was. The star items in the menu were presented, and to the amused surprise of those fellow passengers who were privileged to crowd into the stateroom, the royal travellers manfully, politely and unquestioningly consumed it all. Many such records that appear to be ordinary and matter-of-fact actually tell us only what was strange or unexpected.

Others offer a generalization. No better example can be given than Queen Victoria's breakfast as described in *Royal Chef* (1954), a book based on the reminiscences of Gabriel Tschumi 'as told' in his Wimbledonian retirement 'to Joan Powe':

> Queen Victoria was always up for breakfast, I was told, and had it with one or two members of the Royal Family in the small oak dining-room in the centre of the corridor at Windsor Castle. Rumours had it that her breakfast was usually a boiled egg, served in magnificent style. According to the upper servants, she used a gold egg-cup and a gold spoon . . .
>
> Most of the other members of the Royal Family took breakfast more seriously. They would begin with an egg dish, perhaps Oeuf en cocotte, followed by several rashers of streaky bacon, then grilled trout or turbot, cutlets, chops or steak, and finally a serving of roast woodcock, snipe or chicken.

The 'I was told' might be a warning that Tschumi does not really know, but we can give him the benefit of the doubt here. He got his first post in the Buckingham Palace kitchens thanks to his cousin Louise, one of Queen Victoria's dressers. Even if he didn't observe the queen's daily life at Windsor, Louise certainly did: she was one of those who helped to ensure that the queen was 'up for breakfast'. The real warning is Tschumi's open intention to generalize. All these items were surely served at breakfast, but we don't actually know (at least, not from this quotation or this book) which members of Queen Victoria's family were heavy breakfasters and which of them were the unlucky ones, condemned to face 'a boiled egg, served in magnificent style' at her personal table. We don't know how much they ate of what was served. We don't know whether their breakfasts – or even hers – varied much from day to day. We can easily imagine that tea and coffee were available but we are not told. We may also worry about the fact that Tschumi's story is filtered through a ghost-writer's words, although it seems clear, fortunately for the social historian, that Joan Powe made no attempt to reduce the emphasis on menus and recipes. The result is that a breakfast in *Royal Chef* has much the same persuasive power as a breakfast in a novel, in which the author's aim might be to present an easily believable meal as reassuring background to the improbable twists of the plot.

For a last example let's return to the series of royal ordinances and to one that is slightly earlier than Wolsey's. The *Liber Niger Domus Regis* or 'Black Book of the King's Household', compiled around 1475, focuses on food rather than money.

> The Kyng for his brekefast, two looves made into four maun-
> chetts, and ii payne demayne, one messe of kychyn grosse, dim'
> gallon of ale.

This offers us three important scraps of information. First the varieties of bread: even in this 'private' breakfast there are the lucky few who eat pain-demaine, 'the lord's bread' – the king himself is certainly among them – and the more numerous and less lucky ones who get manchet. Second, half a gallon of ale: an indication that even among the highest in England, whatever Robert Greene and his audience might think, wine was not de rigueur at breakfast. Third, a 'messe of kychyn grosse', that is, a serving of cold meat from the kitchen. The king of this document is to be served leftovers – meat from the previous day's roasting – not bacon or ham or offal. But who is the king? Edward iv himself, one might assume, but this strange document begins with a survey of the households of King Solomon, the mythical King Lud and the scarcely better-known Cassivelaunus. Whether what follows is a real analysis of Edward iv's household or a fictional one is far from clear. As we now see, to the social historian it may not matter very much.

Aside from the contemporary written record, the second source for the history of breakfast is study and comparison. We do it in our minds; anthropologists do it for a living. It gives no new information but it helps us to interpret the information we have. Comparison has already high-lighted the two typical sources of meaty breakfasts: leftovers, meat that was cooked the day before; and salt meat and offal – and this makes us want to question the 'pork and boiled beef' served to Charles ii and the 'cutlets, chops or steak' at Victorian royal breakfasts. Cold or hot? Freshly cooked or reheated?

The third source is – to use its general term – iconography. Break--fasts are almost common enough in nineteenth- and early twentieth-century art to form a genre by themselves: examples appear throughout this book. Recognizing breakfast in earlier genre painting is something of a challenge, but it will repay the effort.

The fourth source is word history. The story of the names of breakfast is a complex one, and it highlights an issue that we have so far managed to avoid, that of the continuing cross-linguistic confusion between breakfast and lunch. We can avoid it no longer.

The Name of Breakfast

The Greeks had two names for it. Or, to put it another way, the Greeks had a name for the last meal of the day, *deipnon*, their biggest meal which we can conveniently translate as 'dinner'; they also had a name for the preceding meal, *ariston*, and they had a name for the quick snack taken at the beginning of the day, *akratisma*. So on the rare occasions when we encounter the word *akratisma* we can always translate it as 'breakfast' – it could never be anything else. But how are we to translate *ariston*? The first thought is 'lunch'. In the quotation from

Ancient Medicine that's how I translated it, as others have before me. In that text the whole discussion seems really to be about main meals and the issue is whether one or two main meals are taken. Clearly, to be understood in modern English, these have to be translated as 'lunch' and 'dinner'. In other texts, however, 'lunch' as the translation of *ariston* doesn't always work. Some narratives make it clear that *ariston* is eaten quite early in the morning. That's how it is with the breakfast in Eumaios' cottage: he and Odysseus 'were preparing *ariston* in the hut as the sun rose'. Sure enough, translators of the *Odyssey* call this meal 'breakfast'. The same is true of the breakfast on the shore of the Sea of Tiberias: 'when dawn came Jesus was standing on the shore' with a fire ready lit and the bread that was wanted for breakfast. 'Come and have *ariston*,' he says soon afterwards. This meal cannot be translated as 'lunch' either: lunch as we know it is taken close to noon, never just after dawn. In this case the translators of John's Gospel are inconsistent: some write 'Come and have breakfast', as I did in my translation above; others, with the feeling that breakfast is not quite biblical enough, prefer to write 'Come and dine', inappropriate though that seems for a meal taken in the first half of the morning. Not one translator writes 'Come and have lunch'. Although lunch is often an accurate translation of *ariston*, it would in this case be as inaccurate as dinner – and feels even less biblical, even more anachronistic, than breakfast.

There is a puzzle here that we haven't yet faced. Why, after all, does *Ancient Medicine* talk about 'one or two meals' as if breakfast didn't even exist – as if no one in ancient Greece ever ate anything before the main meals of the day? But we know they did: there is that Greek word, *akratisma*, a snack taken as soon as one gets up. The real explanation lies in the difference between Mediterranean and northern European lifestyles (and it will turn out that this has something to do with the difference, familiar to all who stay in international hotels, between an *English breakfast* and a *Continental breakfast*). If we trace this difference back to its origin we will finally find the key to the puzzle. In the Mediterranean or 'Continental' style no one eats three solid meals a day. One eats either one or two solid meals a day.

In classical Greek, if there is just one solid meal, it is *deipnon*. If there are two, the first is *āriston*. At a quick glance this word might seem to say that breakfast is best (Greek *ăristos* 'best'), but the long first vowel is a clue that this interpretation would be wrong. *Āriston* ('breakfast') is in fact linked with Greek *ēri* and English *early* and means 'early meal'.

People who worked hard – like the fishermen of the Gospel of John, or Eumaios and his herdsmen – were likely to take *ariston* (they needed it more than anyone else) and might well have it quite early in the day, before mid-morning in fact, having got up and started work before dawn. Those who could afford a more leisurely lifestyle got up later and took their *ariston* later. The later the *ariston* arrived, the more one felt the need for a little something extra first thing in the morning. The little something was called *akratisma*, which means 'a bit of un-mixed' – and that is not as strange a name as it sounds. In ancient Greece wine was usually drunk mixed with water (it lasts longer and is less intoxicating that way) but the early morning *akratisma*, for which

James J. Tissot, 'Christ Appears to his Disciples at the Sea of Tiberias' (from the series *The Life of Christ*), *c.* 1890, opaque watercolour over graphite on grey wove paper. The stranger on the shore has a fire ready for breakfast.

37

a little stimulation was required, typically consisted of a bit of bread with – and soaked in – unmixed wine. Matutinal stimulation in such forms as tea, coffee and chocolate may be something of a novelty, but in other forms it has existed much longer.

Like the Greek *akratisma* the classical Roman breakfast usually consisted of bread and wine, the first often soaked in the last. The names, however, worked differently in Latin. *Cena* was always an evening meal, *prandium* was taken at midday and the quick morning snack was *ientaculum*, 'a bit while fasting' (the Latin adjective *ieiunus* means 'fasting', that is, 'with empty stomach'). The old Latin names for meals haven't wholly disappeared (in Romanian, for example, some people still use the words *prînz* and *cină*) but in northern Italy and southern France, in spite of Latin heritage, habits and names have changed radically. Provençal poetry, from its twelfth-century beginnings, revealed a new word for the biggest meal of the day, and this meal had moved forward to midday or even earlier. 'Who scoffs too long at others' foods will hardly find himself a dinner,' wrote Giraut de Borneil around 1200. There already is the crucial new word, *disnar* – 'dinner'. The time of day at which this dinner was taken is made clear in another poem, the epic *Song of the Albigensian Crusade*. At the battle of Muret in 1213 the men of the south, towards the end of a hard morning, 'undid their belts and sat down to dinner' (*dinnar* – the same new word), unaware that the perfidious northerner Simon de Montfort was leading an attacking luncheon party through the river meadows. King James of Aragon, the southerners' champion, was caught by surprise and killed in battle that afternoon, and all because he took a long late-morning meal.

This *disnar* of the medieval Mediterranean could, of course, be translated as 'lunch' in English. It would work perfectly well that way except that the word feels anachronistic. And so, for the same reason that no one writes 'lunch' when translating the Gospel of John but some are bold enough to write 'breakfast', exactly the same happens when translators have a go at the story of Nastagio degli Onesti in Boccaccio's *Decameron*, which was written in about 1350 in Tuscany. The crisis and dénouement of this story take place around an outdoor meal in the pine woods, and the crucial word – in its Italian form – is the same again, *desinare*. 'Join me in this place for breakfast' is how Nastagio's

Sandro Botticelli, *Nastagio degli Onesti: The Breakfast, c.* 1483, tempera on panel. The breakfasters, to their horror, see an apparently real scene of the hunting down of a naked and defenceless woman. From a series of four paintings illustrating the Nastagio degli Onesti story in the *Decameron*.

invitation appears in a good recent translation, and surely no better word could be found.

Literally, we should understand, this medieval word – Provençal *disnar*, Italian *desinare* and Old French *disner* – has exactly the same sense as the English word *breakfast*: its Latin original is *dis-jejunare* 'to end one's fast'. This is precisely what one did, and the undoing of belts might be required if one took one's main meal not long before midday, having eaten practically nothing since the previous evening. If a quick Mediterranean snack, a bit of bread and a nip of wine, happened to be gulped down before the day began, like the Greek *akratisma* or the Roman *ientaculum*, that didn't count. The fast was not really broken.

With troubadour poetry, which was fashionable throughout medieval Western Europe, this word moved northwards into French, Anglo-Norman and English. But at this point it was caught up in a culture clash. Towards the north, for climatic reasons (one was able to go on working longer through the heat of the day) the main meal was taken

François Boucher, *Le Dejeuner*, 1739, oil on canvas. Boucher is the waiter at this breakfast. Everyone's eyes are on the little girl: it is her first taste of chocolate.

slightly later. Late medieval French *dîner* and English *dinner*, the word so well known from the poets of the south, was applied quite naturally to what was the main meal in the north, a midday or early afternoon meal. But it was not the first meal and it could not even pretend to be such. People in the north needed something more solid inside them as fortification against the chill of the morning. Unlike their Mediterranean neighbours, they were compelled to break their fast definitively, earlier in the day.

What to call that earliest meal of the day, smaller perhaps, but not as small as all that? The answer, oddly enough, was found in the same group of words and meanings. Ask a medieval Frenchman or Englishman what he does when he takes his first meal of the day and the answer will come: *je des-jeune, I break my fast*. Ask him to form an infinitive verb from that expression, and there you will have it: *breakfast, déjeuner*.

In French, then, through the centuries-long history of the word, *dîner* has always been the name for the main meal of the northern French day, and never for the first meal of the day. Its place on the timetable has shifted, however. In Paris before the Revolution, in rural areas even more recently and in Quebec to this day, *dîner* was and is taken soon after noon. To those who did it that way, the smaller, evening meal that followed was known as *souper*, literally 'to drink soup', and the small meal taken at the beginning of the day was *déjeuner*. After the Revolution the main meal, *dîner*, shifted to later in the day (allegedly because the busy politicians of revolutionary Paris were hard at work legislating until late in the afternoon). This shift eventually obliterated *souper*, which is now rarely taken as a separate meal, and it brought with it a change for *déjeuner* which also crept to a later slot and became a midday meal, much larger and (except for busy politicians) more leisurely than it ever was before. In turn this created, all over again, the need for a small meal taken early in the day; hence the origin and name of *petit déjeuner*, the 'little *déjeuner*', which now keeps the French digestive system satisfied until *déjeuner* arrives.

Translating French texts from before the Revolution presents no problem. *Déjeuner, dîner, souper* are 'breakfast', 'dinner', 'supper' and the reader needs only a gentle reminder that for these French people, as for their English contemporaries, dinner was a midday meal. Likewise, the translation of Parisian French from the late nineteenth century onwards is also without difficulty. *Petit déjeuner, déjeuner, dîner* are 'breakfast', 'lunch', 'dinner', as we learned at school, and no one is surprised. However, during the period of the changeover – the first half of the nineteenth century in Paris right up to the present day in Quebec, and until very recently, at least, in rural France and Belgium – the translator can't apply a fixed rule. Depending on time, place and social milieu, *dîner* may be eaten any time between midday and mid-evening. *Déjeuner* may be breakfast or it may be lunch. *Souper* may or may not survive. *Petit déjeuner* may or may not have been invented.

Luckily the confusion over the name of breakfast in recent French doesn't exist in most other languages. In English, for example, while *dinner* has travelled to later in the day, just as it has in French, and *supper* has largely been squeezed out, a newer word, *luncheon* or *lunch*, originally a mid-morning snack, had by the mid-nineteenth century become standard for the midday meal that has now generally supplanted the early *dinner*. The English name for the smaller meal taken at the beginning of the day, *breakfast*, simply wasn't affected by any of this. The word is the same today as it was in the fifteenth century. It's interesting, but not surprising, that all three of the older English meal names are taken from French. *Dinner* and *supper* are obvious, but *breakfast*, too, was directly patterned on *déjeuner* at the period when French and English had jostled for status as England's national language. In fact *déjeuner* was sometimes explained in French, by Laurent Joubert in 1586 for example, as *rompre la jeûne* – 'break the fast'.

The idea of 'breaking a fast' was around in England long before the Norman Conquest, with the Anglo-Saxon noun *fæstenbryce*, but this meant literally the breach of a relig us fast and not an early morning meal. The phrase, to *break* one's *fast*, occurs in a more everyday context some time after the year 1400 in *The Tale of Beryn*, an amusing anonymous sequel to Chaucer's *Canterbury Tales*. On the pilgrims' arrival in Canterbury the pardoner fraternizes with a 'tapster' or barmaid. 'Sit down, ye shall drink!' she tells him. At first he is reluctant to eat: he is still fasting, having not yet worshipped at St Thomas à Becket's shrine. She knows a cure for that, however, and goes out to buy him a hot pie. 'Eat and be merry,' she urges, 'why break ye not your fast?' Whatever

Édouard Manet, *Le Déjeuner dans l'atelier*, 1868, oil on canvas. 'Lunch in the studio', according to some, but the coffee-pot suggests breakfast.

exactly the flirtatious tapster meant by that, it is evident from other texts that a century later one could perfectly well *break* one's *fast* in English by taking a morning meal after an ordinary overnight fast: there need be no implication of religious observance. Sir Anthony Fitzherbert's 1523 advice to farmers makes this quite clear:

> Specially in winter-time, when thou sittest by the fire and hast supped . . . go to thy bed and sleep, and be up betime, and break thy fast before day, that thou mayest be all the short winter's day about thy business. At grammar school I learned a verse that is this:
>
> *Sanat, sanctificat et ditat surgere mane,*
>
> that is to say, 'Early rising maketh a man whole in body, wholer in soul and richer in goods.'

The Latin tag on early rising, quoted by Fitzherbert here to back up his advice, is one to which we shall return.

A survey of other languages brings to light a range of senses out of which names for breakfast are commonly extracted. Often an influential neighbouring culture will lend a name. Modern French *petit déjeuner*, interpreted as 'little lunch', suggested two Romanian terms: *prînzişor*, the diminutive of *prandium*, the old, originally Latin, name for 'lunch'; and *mic dejun*, which adopts the modern French word for 'lunch' and adds the little Romanian adjective 'little'. Portuguese *pequeno almoço* has exactly the same literal meaning – 'little lunch'.

Portuguese also has the verb *desjejuar*, 'to end one's fast', and the noun *desjejum*. Spanish has *desayunarse* and *desayuno*, and Catalan has the noun *desdejuni*. All are exactly parallel to the French *déjeuner*. Another Portuguese term is *quebra-jejum*, quite literally 'break-fast'. English, exerting a heavy influence on its neighbours, gave its name *breakfast* almost unadapted to Welsh *brecwast*, Scottish Gaelic *bracaist* and Irish *bricfeast*.

An unrecorded early medieval Latin term *admordium*, 'a bite', was clearly the origin of words that are used for 'breakfast' in some parts of the Iberian peninsula and for 'lunch' in others. Hence breakfast is *almozo* in Galician, *almuerzo* in certain Spanish-speaking regions, *almusal* in Tagalog and *esmorzar* in Catalan, yet in ordinary Spanish *almuerzo* is 'lunch'. The same Latin word could also have been the inspiration for the German name for 'breakfast', *Frühstück*, literally 'an early bit or bite'.

The German term, on the other hand, is also reminiscent of words in neighbouring languages: on one side the Dutch *ontbijt* (and the older German *Imbiss*), 'a bite'; on the other the Norwegian and Swedish names, *frokost* and *frukost*, 'early meal', a term also recorded in north German dialects which has exactly the same sense as the Greek *ariston* with which we began. The German dialect term was borrowed into Latvian, a Baltic language that shows many signs of German trade and conquest. The modern Latvian word, still recognizably German, is *bruokastis*.

The Italian *colazione* is of different origin, implying a meal put together from food that was already prepared and ready to eat. This word is used by some Greek speakers in the form *kolatsió*. The fuller form of the Italian term, *prima colazione*, brings in a different series of meanings: it reminds us that breakfast is the first such meal, and therefore the 'first meal' of the day. Another, Irish term, *céadbhéile*, also means 'first meal'.

A common Malay name is *makan pagi*, 'morning meal'. This pattern, too, repeats elsewhere: in Japanese *asa-gohan*, for example, and in Vietnamese *bữa ăn sáng*. It is found in Swiss-German *Morgenessen*, Danish *morgenmad*, Icelandic *morgunmatur* and Anglo-Saxon *morȝenmete* – one of the two really old English words (for the second, see below) for the first meal of the day that were ousted under the Normans by the newfangled *breakfast*. These in turn are parallel to Breton *pred-beure*, Welsh *boreubryd*, Scottish Gaelic *biadh-maidne* and Irish *béile na maidne*, all four meaning 'morning meal'.

Similar again is modern Greek *proinó*, literally 'the morning one', which is paralleled by Swiss-German *Zmorge*, Finnish *aamiainen* and by

Hugo Birger, *Skandinaviska konstnärernas frukost i Café Ledoyen*, 1886, oil on canvas. Annual breakfast of the Scandinavian artists in Paris at the Café Ledoyen on the Champs-Elysées.

a common Russian, Slovene and Serbian-Croatian word for 'breakfast', *zayutrak, zajtrk, zavtrak*, literally 'at morning'. An additional Serbian-Croatian term is *doručak*, 'beside or until the meal': this is reminiscent of the Polish *śniadanie*, Czech *snídaně*, Belorussian *snyadanak*, Ukrainian *snidanok* – 'with or alongside the meal'.

Not so very different from these is the old Gothic word *undaurnimats*, used in the Gothic translation of the New Testament, which is exactly parallel to the second of the two Anglo-Saxon words, *undernmete*. These Gothic and Anglo-Saxon compounds meant literally 'the meal taken at undern, the third hour of the day', or nine o'clock in our terms. Since the Goths migrated southwards from the Baltic shores, it is not too surprising that the Lithuanian word still in use today is almost identical in meaning: *pusryčiai*, 'half-morning or mid-morning meal'. In Sanskrit literature a similarly specific word is found, though the exact meaning is different: *prātarācas* – 'eating in the early morning'.

These endless variations suggest how unproductive it would be to try to reconstruct early names for breakfast in proto-Indo-European or other ancestral languages. As habits and fashions change and new ways of life lead to different daily timetables, people's mealtimes change and so do their names for meals – hence the many cases above in which two or even three or four alternative terms for breakfast are found in the same language, some perhaps old-fashioned, some newfangled, some regional or dialectal.

What we can do, though, is point to repeating patterns. It is likely enough that when Neolithic peoples settled into a routine that included breakfast, different communities devised different names for it, such as 'the early morning meal' (as they would call it in Sanskrit in the far future), or 'mid-morning meal' (as in Lithuanian and Anglo-Saxon), or just 'morning meal' (as in Gaelic, Swedish, Finnish, Russian, Malay and Japanese). Or perhaps they would name it after the beverage that formed part of it – 'morning drink' or 'early morning drink', or perhaps naming the specific drink that was chosen. So it would be in classical Greek with *akratisma*, the 'sip of unmixed wine'; so it would be in the French dialects of Belgium, *café-déjeuner* – the 'lunch that consists mainly of coffee'; in Brazilian Portuguese, *café da manhã* – 'morning coffee'; and in the creole of Cabo Verde, simply *café* – 'coffee'. In modern

Greek, too, there is *kafes* – literally 'coffee'; in Russian some say *chay* – 'tea'; in Turkish many say *kahvaltı* – 'six o'clock coffee'. Or perhaps the chosen term might be something more expressive: breaking the fast, as people were to say in French, Spanish and English, or killing the worm, *mata-bicho*, as they were to say in the Portuguese of Angola and Mozambique. One would imagine it is not a literal worm – more a metaphorical beast that gnaws at the hungry stomach.

The Marchioness of Montferrat's chicken breakfast from an illuminated manuscript of the *Decameron*, Italian, 15th century.

two

Breakfast
Through Time

> That tea is a luxury, and not a fit aliment for the poor, is
> implied in a sarcasm of Swift to this purpose: that the world
> must be encompassed, that is to say, by a voyage to the East
> Indies for tea, and another to the West for sugar, before a
> washerwoman can sit down to breakfast.
>
> John Hawkins, *The Life of Samuel Johnson, Ll.D.* (London, 1787)

L et's start at the beginning. The earliest breakfasts hinted at in the
written record anywhere in the world are those of the Egyptian
pharaohs, who employed a palace official with the dignified title of
'Supervisor of the King's Breakfast'. The Egyptian word for breakfast
was a surprising one: *ja.w-r'*, means literally 'mouth-cleansing'. We
know from occasional texts the typical constituents of this mouth-
cleansing: only partly liquid, generally consisting of bread soaked in
wine – one of the more nourishing ways to wash one's mouth. Here,
already, is a typical Mediterranean quick breakfast taken in the early
morning. It serves as a reminder that in Mediterranean lands at later
periods we find two different meals for which our obvious name has
to be breakfast.

We have already encountered the two Greek names. *Akratisma*,
to the ancient Greeks, was just what the Egyptians would have called
ja.w-r'. It was this word that came to the mind of some later readers
when they tried to picture what was going on in Eumaios' hut. The poet
called it *ariston*, but that seemed an unsatisfactory term. 'The poet is
talking about the snack taken at dawn', writes Athenaios, third-century

scholar of ancient food. 'We call this *akratisma*, of course, because the bits of bread are dunked in unmixed wine.' Athenaios continues with a couple of quotations from later Athenian comedies which conveniently show the two words, for two kinds of breakfast, in use side by side.

A: The cook's preparing *ariston*.
B: Then how about having an *akratisma* with me?

That is from Antiphanes. Next, from a contemporary playwright, Kantharos, two travellers thinking about food:

A: Aren't we having our *akratisma* here?
B: Not a bit of it. We're on our way to *ariston* at the Isthmus.

And then, from a third playwright, Aristomenes, a reminder of what exactly the *akratisma* contains: 'I'll have a little *akratisma*, just two or three bits of bread, and I'll be there.'

Athenaios was not the only scholar to be puzzled by the *ariston* that Eumaios and Odysseus were getting ready at dawn. The question had also been discussed, a century earlier, around the dinner table of the scholar Plutarch. 'We decided that the *ariston* is the same as an *akratisma*', he reports in *Table Talk*, 'on the evidence of Homer, who says that Eumaios and crew "were preparing breakfast in the hut as the sun rose".' Plutarch and Athenaios forgot that Eumaios is running a mountain farm. His labourers are out at work before dawn and will want more solid sustenance than a bit of bread dunked in wine; hence *ariston* at Eumaios' is something more than an *akratisma*.

But Plutarch is also the earliest writer (he lived around AD 100) to perceive and state clearly the big distinction between breakfast and other meals that we saw in chapter One. 'People took *ariston* wherever they were, simply and without any great trouble, using what happened to be available.' This is indeed the true nature of breakfast: in Eumaios' case it is the 'roast meat that had been left uneaten the day before'; at breakfast in *The Grapes of Wrath* it's the salt pork or 'side-meat' taken from store. It's different on the one hand from an *akratisma*, which is just a bit of bread and wine; different on the other from a dinner, which is (ideally at any rate) newly cooked from fresh ingredients.

In Latin only one word is relevant – *ientaculum*. Admittedly *prandium* was the Latin word used to translate Greek *ariston*, but a proper Latin *prandium* was always taken later in the day, around noon or after, and we have no choice but to call it 'lunch'. Romans took their breakfast, *ientaculum*, a little less seriously than a Greek *ariston* but a little more seriously than an *akratisma*. The epigrammatist Martial, in a verse written to accompany a Saturnalia gift, makes the individuality of Roman breakfast habits clear:

> *Si sine carne voles ientacula sumere frugi,*
> *Haec tibi Vestino de grege massa venit.*

> If you wish to enjoy a meat-free breakfast,
> this product of the kneading-trough comes to you from the
>   Vestini.

Not just a loaf of bread, that is, but one that has been kneaded and baked in the gastronomically approved style of the Vestini of central Italy. So, if Martial's verse makes any psychological sense, a Roman might take *ientaculum* with or without meat, which sets it somewhere between the Greek *akratisma* and *ariston* (or, if it comes to that, somewhere between the Continental and English breakfast). The emperor Vitellius, according to his disgusted biographer Suetonius, managed to feast immoderately four times a day, *in iantacula et prandia et cenas comisationesque* – 'at breakfasts, lunches, dinners and late night revels' – thanks to his habit of vomiting. It follows that others around Vitellius must also have taken a somewhat bigger breakfast than the venerable bit of bread dunked in wine, even if no one around him ate quite as uncontrollably as he did.

For our knowledge of another important ingredient of the Roman breakfast we must thank the lifelike atmosphere of the fantasy novel *Metamorphoses* by Apuleius. The story opens with a traveller's tale: a journey on foot through northern Greece and a disturbed night at the inn at Hypata. From here the storyteller sets out early with one travelling companion who, after a few miles, suddenly weakens.

> 'My knees are shaking and my feet are stumbling and if I'm to recover I need something to eat.'
> 'Look here,' I told him, 'I have a breakfast ready for you.'
> I took my pack off my shoulder and handed him a cheese and a loaf of bread. I said: 'Let's sit down under that plane tree.'
> I started to eat something myself and I watched him munching greedily . . . Anyway, after polishing off the food he was suddenly very thirsty, naturally enough, because he had greedily eaten the best part of a first-rate cheese.

This hungry fellow traveller soon comes to a sticky end, but never mind that. In reaching this point Apuleius has given us a typical Roman traveller's *ientaculum*. In Greek terms (they are in Greece, after all) this isn't the *akratisma* – the bit of bread and wine that they might have taken before leaving the inn – but the more solid *ariston* that they had earned after travelling a certain number of miles. There's no meat; cheese is more convenient to travellers and it's something that this particular narrator (a cheese merchant) is always likely to have in his pack.

Some time during the later Roman Empire, a shift in mealtimes took place in Mediterranean lands, or at any rate a shift in perception of mealtimes, which henceforth matched Greek categories rather than Roman ones. There is no room here to explore the reasons but the chief result was that the Latin word *prandium*, 'lunch', fell out of fashion. It was replaced, more or less, by the medieval word *desinare* or *disnar* whose long-term fate we traced in chapter One. This newly named meal was taken earlier in the day than the Latin *prandium*: it was a mid-morning meal corresponding to the Greek *ariston*. Once again, therefore, in following the history of Mediterranean breakfasts, we have two meals to account for. The fuller mid-morning meal, which might well include meat or cheese, was the Greek *ariston* reborn as *desinare*. The early-morning snack, a bit of bread and wine, so quick and light that many people didn't think of it as a meal, was the Greek *akratisma*.

Thanks to a medieval source with an atmosphere just as lifelike as that in *Metamorphoses* – Boccaccio's *Decameron* – we can see both kinds of breakfast in their rightful context. I've already mentioned the breakfast (*desinare*) offered by Nastagio degli Onesti to his unfriendly beloved but it's not the only example in the *Decameron*. In the course of a tightly negotiated affair between the pretty Belcolore and her village priest, the latter, scheming to get back the cloak he has unwisely left in her room and which she is keeping hostage, begs the loan of her stone mortar because he is to *desinare* the next morning with two friends and wants to prepare a *salsa*. The following day he sends the mortar back when Belcolore is at breakfast and asks for the cloak 'that he had left as security'. Unable to refuse in front of her husband, Belcolore replies angrily that he won't be grinding any more *salsa* in her mortar, but the priest has an answer to that: if she won't let him have her mortar, she certainly won't see any more of his pestle. A third *desinare* is that prepared by the Marchioness of Montferrat for

The baker Cisti, from an illuminated manuscript of the *Decameron*, French translation, 15th century.

King Philip of France, who is travelling to Genoa on crusade and hopes to seduce her on the way. He invites himself to *desinare*, and the countess, guessing what he has in mind, orders a very special breakfast for him.

> After he had rested briefly in his apartment the time came to *desinare*: the king and the marchioness sat at one table and the rest at other tables according to their rank. Served with various dishes and with fine and costly wines, and constantly regaled with the sight of the beautiful marchioness, the king was very happy, but then he noticed, as one dish followed another, that although they were different, they were all chicken . . .
>
> 'Madam,' he said, 'are there only chickens in this country? No cocks?'

He is asking for a put-down and he gets one. But what of the meal? Translators hesitate in this instance, sometimes calling it a lunch, sometimes even a banquet, although Boccaccio uses the term that translates as 'breakfast' elsewhere. But there's no need for hesitation: although elaborate in one sense, this meal is very breakfastish in the simplicity of its menu – and in another important way. The king has been travelling and a solid breakfast, in both reality and literature, is the reward one gets after setting out early on a journey.

Alongside these rather large breakfasts, Boccaccio also gives us a rare description of the other, lighter, even more typical Mediterranean breakfast in its medieval form. This can be found in the story of the Florentine baker Cisti (a real historical figure, incidentally), who enjoys the best wine and likes to share good things with others but is not quite brave enough to issue an invitation to his vastly wealthy fellow citizen, Geri Spini, Pope Boniface VIII's banker. And so:

> Every morning, at the time when he was sure that Geri Spini and the Papal emissaries would be passing, he would have set out in front of his door a shiny new jug of fresh water and a little new Bolognese carafe of his best white wine and two goblets that were so shiny that they looked like silver. Then he would

sit down at the table, and as Spini and his visitors were going by he would cough to clear his throat a couple of times and would begin to sip this wine of his with such enjoyment that it would almost have made a corpse thirsty.

When Geri Spini had observed this for a couple of days, on the third morning he said:

'What's it like, Cisti? Is it good?'

Cisti jumped to his feet and said:

'It is, sir, but I'll never make you understand how good it is unless you try it.'

This meal (to which Boccaccio gives no name) consists of good wine and good bread, or so we may assume, since the breakfaster is a baker. And Cisti takes the opportunity to clear his throat – to cleanse his mouth, in other words. No change, then: this is the *ientaculum* of ancient Rome, the light *akratisma* of ancient Greece and the *ja.w-r'*, the 'mouth-cleansing' of ancient Egypt.

In all other medieval and early modern texts from Mediterranean countries the full, mid-morning breakfast predominates. Alongside the *Song of the Albigensian Crusade* (quoted in chapter One) one other medieval Provençal narrative describes what might reasonably be called a breakfast. It's a meal with no name, but it happens before the main work of the day has begun and after a journey that the poet carelessly dismisses as short: Olivier has ridden in from Roncesvalles to join King Charlemagne's troops at Saragossa in readiness for battle.

> *Es Olivier vay mangier demandant:*
> *Un gran signe li aporton davant,*
> *Blancs fogassetz e vin clar e pumant;*
> *Aqui manget a qui venc ha talant . . .*

Olivier demands food. They set before him a fat swan, white *fogassetz* and *clairet* wine and spiced wine; all comers eat what they want. When he has eaten, up he gets. They bring the warhorse and rub him down; they set before him seven handfuls of oats and let him eat as much of it as he wants.

The swan makes it an unusual breakfast, we may think, but Olivier is after all a legendary hero and *Roland at Saragossa* is an epic poem. Likewise spiced wine is surprising at breakfast but commonplace in descriptions of medieval epic meals. But light red wine, *vin clar*, will do nicely for breakfast; so will those *fogassetz* (or *fouaces* or *focaccie*). Not unlike Olivier, modern Italian schoolchildren may buy a slice of *focaccia* on the way to school for their mid-morning snack.

Moving on to Spain, there are many inns and many meals in Cervantes' *Don Quixote* but few identifiable breakfasts. On one of their many journeys Don Quixote and Sancho restore themselves after a morning encounter with a herd of bulls. The result is a travellers' breakfast very similar to the one described by Apuleius above.

> In a clear and limpid spring, which they found in a shady clump of trees, Don Quixote and Sancho . . . sat down to rest from their fatigue, leaving Dapple and Rocinante loose without headstall or bridle. Sancho had recourse to the larder in his saddle-bags, and brought out what he called relish [*condumio*]. He rinsed his mouth, and Don Quixote washed his face . . . The squire silently, and in defiance of all the rules of good breeding, began to cram the bread and cheese into his mouth.

The relish – food to accompany bread – and the mouth-rinsing are concepts now familiar to us. One suspects that Sancho's mouth-rinsing requires wine, but this is not made explicit. Cheese, for Sancho as for Apuleius' narrator, is more practical than meat when considered as a relish to store in a traveller's pack.

As if to excuse his rudeness in beginning to eat before his master, Sancho goes on to quote a fatalistic proverb against himself (*Muera Marta, y muera harta*, 'Martha will die, and she'll die stuffed'); he and the reader may recall a less fatal variant (*Bien canta Marta despues de harta*, 'Martha sings well once she's stuffed').

We noted in chapter One that in the cold medieval north the solid early meal known in the south as *disnar* was taken later in the day – in northern France, for example, *diner* was generally consumed towards noon or later. As such it has no part in this story. Medieval and early modern Frenchmen needed to break their fasts before this, and they called the resulting early meal *déjeuner*. And then, as we saw above, *déjeuner* itself began to change. The gourmet Grimod de la Reynière, ironic participant in this gastronomic adventure, had at least two attempts to make sense of what was going on. In the February section of his landmark annual *Almanach des gourmands*, volume 1 (1803), he tells it thus:

> *Déjeuner* is an inconsequential meal. A man who prefers not to display his wealth, a bachelor who has no household staff, a modest gastronome – all these can give a breakfast without shocking their neighbours or arousing gossip. Women are usually not invited; starting early gives the jaws more time to do their work; a lively morning appetite can be fully satisfied without risk to health, and for all these reasons mastication is the principal object of these gatherings . . .

I omit the avalanches of food, wine, coffee, brandy, ice cream and liqueurs that Grimod then enumerates for his 'inconsequential meal'. He continues: 'These late *déjeuners*, of which we have given the merest sketch, are far different from those of our fathers, who confined themselves to a few cups of *café à la crême* or *chocolat à la vanille*; even if they wanted to grease their knives (so to speak) a slice of Bayonne ham or a bit of Italian cheese was enough to satisfy them,' though not enough to satisfy Grimod himself, who mentions additional relishes that his predecessors may or may not have taken. Now comes the punchline:

> The Revolution has changed everything in France, even to its stomachs, which have gained digestive capacities previously unknown. It must be agreed that if this were the only kind of change the Revolution had effected many people would be less inclined to complain about it.

This was the best that Grimod could do at his first attempt. *Déjeuner* – 'breakfast' – as he described it had become a large and long meal, one that particularly lent itself to entertaining at Carnival time. But he wasn't satisfied, and came back to the subject in volume II (1804). Too late, perhaps, it had occurred to him that a crucial change – in the daily timetable – had not yet been mentioned. 'Working habits at our businesses and banking houses are different nowadays,' he wrote, and went on:

> The result is that we take *dîner* at a later hour than they used to take *souper* in king Charles VIII's time, and our *déjeuner* has become a large meal. A cup of tea or lime tea – or even coffee with milk the way they make it in Paris – will not last you until dinner if dinner hardly ever arrives before six in the evening.

Some of Grimod's contemporaries, meanwhile, saw no reason to change their habits. The great diplomat Talleyrand, who triumphantly survived these interesting times, took the same breakfasts at the end of his life as he did at the beginning: he 'usually rose about ten or eleven . . . and about half an hour afterwards made a light breakfast of eggs and fish, and Madeira mixed with water. He never drank coffee, chocolate or tea in the morning.' By the time of his death in 1838 at the age of 85 he was a museum piece. Frenchwomen – and even Frenchmen if they were not as rich as Grimod's bankers – had by then taken to chocolate as a nourishing breakfast alternative to the older-established coffee and tea. If they were feeling feeble it might even be 'the renowned fortifying chocolate, light yet nutritious, prepared with Persian *salep*' to which Grimod gave especial praise. Although the phrase *petit déjeuner* was unknown to him (it was not thought of until 1866 or thereabouts) Grimod was the faithful chronicler who traced for us the establishment of the trinity – *café, thé, chocolat* – that still comprises every adult's choice of beverage for *petit déjeuner* in twenty-first-century France.

We can identify breakfast in Britain only from the moment that medieval *ientaculum* or *déjeuner* crossed the Channel (although Anglo-Saxon names for breakfast existed, no such meal is ever described). There were *ientacula* in England in the late thirteenth century and plenty of documented *breakfasts* by the early fifteenth. Over several centuries the regular menu changed little: there was bread, and ale or beer, and cheese or boiled beef or, on fast days, salt fish. The *Liber Niger Domus Regis*, the idealized household book of Edward IV's court, sternly prescribes distinctions by rank – bread, meat and ale for breakfast at the king's table, and fixed amounts in descending order for the daily meals of a queen, a duke, a marquess, a count and a bishop – but there is not one tasty detail. From other incidental sources we have the umbles of a deer and the hot pie quoted earlier. Setting these aside, it is Shakespeare, no less, who brings to light one more of the great constituents of an English breakfast, dismissed by Falstaff in a throwaway phrase, 'Grace thou wilt have none . . . No, by my troth, not so much as will serve to be prologue to an egg and butter.' A short grace, or rather, no grace at all, needs to be said before such a minor meal as breakfast. If the meaning is uncertain in Act I Scene 2 of *Henry IV Part 1*, the doubt is settled in Act II Scene 1, in which overnight lodgers at an inn are said to be 'up already, and call for eggs and butter, and will be away presently'. This leaves no doubt that eggs and butter – as 'relish' accompanying the obvious bread and ale – are a normal breakfast at a Shakespearian tavern.

The fullest information on early modern English breakfasts comes from Samuel Pepys's diary. When chronicling his breakfasts he gives us not only the menu but the place, time and company. At home in London he sometimes took breakfast on his way to the office and sometimes, at least, shared it with others: 'This morning Mr Sheply and I did eat our breakfasts at Mrs Harpers, my brother John being with me, upon a cold turkey pie and a goose.' This is early January 1660, and 'Mrs Harper's' is a tavern in King Street, Westminster, almost opposite Axe Yard where Pepys lived. The turkey pie and goose were obviously on the dinner menu the previous evening: breakfast at Mrs Harper's consists of the leftovers. Mr Shipley, Edward Mountagu's steward, is Pepys's close colleague. Pepys is about to accompany his younger brother John to Cambridge to see him settled at Christ's College.

Later the same month, on his way back from Cambridge, Pepys stays overnight at Epping, then: 'Up in the morning, and had some red herrings to our breakfast while my boot-heel was a-mending.' If his boot had not needed mending he would probably have set out earlier and taken breakfast on the road or not at all. As it was, he ate what the unnamed inn had available, not so very far removed from what we would now call kippers.

Pepys and Mountagu sail to Holland in May 1660 among the party that will escort Charles II and his two brothers back to England. On the outward voyage Pepys records 'a breakfast of radyshes at the purser's cabin', and on the return the unusual breakfast served to the three royal passengers (quoted in chapter One). Five days later, the vessel now coasting Kent, Pepys has an unexpected treat: 'About 8 a-clock in the morning, the Lieutenant came to me to know whether I would eat a dish of mackrell, newly-ketched this morning, for my breakfast – which the Captain and we did in the coach' – the 'coach' being the Captain's apartment.

Breakfasts are fewer in the succeeding months and years of Pepys's diary, perhaps because he generally took no breakfast. That, at least, is the view of his modern editor Robert Latham. On a visit to Cambridgeshire long after he had given up his diary, however, Pepys took breakfast on medical advice to protect himself against the 'fenny ague'.

Latham comments on a different term found occasionally in the diary: 'He often took a *morning draught*, often with a snack, at midmorning.' Latham firmly distinguishes *morning draught* from breakfast; his analysis might be right, but Pepys himself makes me doubt it, and a quotation from the diary entry for 22 September 1660 shows why:

> We walked on to Fleetstreet, where at Mr Standing's in Salisbury Court we drank our morning draught and had a pickled herring. Among other discourse here, he told me how the pretty woman that I always loved at the beginning of Cheapside . . . [had been lured into prostitution. After this gossip] . . . to Westminster to my Lord's; and there in the house of office vomited up all my breakfast, my stomach being ill all this day by reason of the last night's debauch.

There is no other mention of breakfast in this day's entry. When the human digestive system is 'ill', what goes down last comes up first, so the 'house of office' or jakes took delivery of Pepys's morning draught and pickled herring, and it must be this that he calls his breakfast.

Diego Velázquez, *Breakfast*, *c.* 1618, oil on canvas.

Therefore Pepys's mid-morning snack, as a separate event, does not exist. Occasional mentions of an English *morning draught* by other authors around Pepys's time lead to the same conclusion. It isn't a mid-morning snack. It might sometimes be an early morning drink before a later breakfast, but it might more often be breakfast itself under another aspect.

One later use of the same phrase gives it the early morning sense. This is in George Borrow's narrative of travels in Andalucia in 1836, *The Bible in Spain*. Borrow is sleeping on a bench in a cheap tavern at Bonanza, the harbour of Sanlúcar de Barrameda, awaiting the ferry that will call at four a.m.

I was awakened more than once during the night by cats, and
I believe rats, leaping upon my body . . . it was half-past three
o'clock. I opened the door and looked out; whereupon some
fishermen entered clamouring for their morning draught: the
old man was soon on his feet serving them.

This *morning draught*, as Borrow calls it, is bread soaked in wine (if
indeed there is any bread): it may have much or little to do with English
breakfast habits but, consumed before dawn, it is certainly the early, light
breakfast or mouth-cleansing of the ancient and medieval Mediterranean, still flourishing.

In the two centuries that followed Samuel Pepys's lifetime, the
everyday British breakfast became simpler, lighter and more predictable. There was often no relish at all to go with the bread, or none but
butter. That is the custom outlined by the Spanish traveller Manuel
Gonzalez, who was in England in 1730: 'A breakfast of coffee, tea, or
chocolate, with bread and butter, a flesh dinner, and a spare supper, is
the common practice.' Not long afterwards an Irish painter, a friend of
Samuel Johnson from Birmingham days, wrote to advise Johnson how
little money a man needed to survive in London: 'By spending threepence in a coffee-house, he might be for some hours every day in very
good company; he might dine for sixpence, breakfast on bread and
milk for a penny, and do without supper.' A century later there were
even better breakfasts, with butter added to the bread and milk to the
coffee, still on sale in London for a penny. At Rodway's coffee-house,
beside the great fish market at Billingsgate, so Henry Mayhew recorded
in 1851, 'a man can have a meal for 1d. – a mug of hot coffee and two slices
of bread and butter, while for two-pence what is elegantly termed "a tight-
ner", that is to say, a most plentiful repast, may be obtained.' Rodway's
clients, 1,500 of them each working day, were not alone in demanding
this modest English breakfast with nothing more than butter accompanying the bread – Edward Lear admitted to the same choice (in hexameters,
in a private poem), though he preferred tea to coffee:

Washing my rose-coloured flesh and brushing my beard
with a hairbrush, / Breakfast of tea, bread-and-butter, at

nine o'clock in the morning, / Sending my carpetbag
onward I reached the Twickenham station . . .

Other English breakfasts in the realm of fiction or memoir, though
less modest than this, are still modest enough. Hot rolls were a luxurious
replacement for sliced bread, but eggs (and of course butter) were suffi-
cient relish when Thomas Babington Macaulay was invited to breakfast
at Holland House in 1831, and he was perfectly satisfied, listing 'very
good coffee, and very good tea, and very good eggs, butter kept in the
midst of ice, and hot rolls'. A rasher of bacon, certainly one of the
canonical choices, is good enough as relish for Mr George and Phil in
Dickens's *Bleak House*:

> Phil, raising a powerful odour of hot rolls and coffee, prepares
> breakfast . . . It is not necessarily a lengthened preparation,
> being limited to the setting forth of very simple breakfast
> requisites for two and the broiling of a rasher of bacon at the
> fire in the rusty grate.

Edmund Gosse in his 'The Poet at the Breakfast Table', another
private poem, names one relish and it is a good one: mackerel. Or are
there two?

> In rose-lit air and light perfume,
> The well-appointed breakfast-room
> Delights us as we tread the stair . . .
> But most I love the sticky stare
> Of pickled mackerel, grand and dumb,
>   In rows.
> And while these dainties we consume
> Let educated youth prepare,
> Flushed with new science like a bloom,
> In our rapt hearing to declare,
> How many little eggs there are
>   In roes.

Are the eggs (or roe) a second relish, or merely a topic of academic conversation? Austin Dobson, the first reader of this poem, which was sent to him in a letter of 1877, had to work that out for himself. Gosse's title cheekily acknowledges Oliver Wendell Holmes's conversation-piece *The Poet at the Breakfast-table*, published five years earlier.

Is this an acceptable picture of nineteenth- and early twentieth-century breakfast in England? It is according to the mid-Edwardian edition of Mrs Isabella Beeton's *Book of Household Management*. The author was long dead but her book remained a bible, and its 'Economical family breakfasts for a week' suggests one or two savouries per day. The daily menus are laboriously set out, with every day the same ('marmalade, butter, toast, bread, coffee, tea, hot and cold milk') except for the savouries with which each day's menu begins: boiled eggs and cold bacon on Sunday, findon haddock on Monday, scrambled eggs and beef roll on Tuesday, fish cakes on Wednesday and on to the broiled fresh herrings and boiled eggs of Saturday. If families chose a more economical breakfast than this (as hundreds of thousands certainly did) they had better not waste any money on Mrs Beeton.

Across the Irish Sea, one relish on any one day is enough for James Joyce's hero, Leopold Bloom, and he takes some trouble to get it. On the day on which the reader of *Ulysses* follows him (see chapter Five) it is to be his favourite grilled mutton kidney, the last remaining in the window at Dlugacz the butcher's.

Was one relish sufficiently solid to stir George Orwell's fascinated disdain? In 'England Your England' (1941) he wrote that 'there is something distinctive and recognizable in English civilization. It is a culture as individual as that of Spain. It is somehow bound up with solid breakfasts and gloomy Sundays . . .'

Or perhaps the breakfast of Orwell's imagination was closer to that enjoyed by the three men in a boat of Jerome K. Jerome's novel of 1889 when planning their journey: they 'sat down to chops and cold beef. Harris said: "The great thing is to make a good breakfast," and he started with a couple of chops, saying that he would take these while they were hot, as the beef could wait.'

But in early nineteenth-century England, breakfast had begun to display the strange dichotomy that still affects our mental image of this

Zinaida Serebryakova, *Breakfast*, 1914, oil on canvas.

first meal of the day. It is this that we will now explore. There is no single British breakfast, and for about two centuries there has not been any single British breakfast. There are two. One is the breakfast that people usually take; the other is the breakfast that they dream of and call 'Great'. They know people who remember, they themselves might occasionally approach, they nearly always can't face, yet they are sure that for patriotic reasons they ought to be eating, a 'Great British Breakfast'. Might it even be true (as Eileen White asserted in 1994) that 'any visitor to this country expects to start the day with bacon, eggs and sausages, perhaps accompanied by tomatoes or mushrooms, and followed by toast and marmalade'?

The appearance in literature of the Great breakfast can be dated quite accurately. As noted by Kaori O'Connor in *The English Breakfast*

A French officer breakfasts with English officers during the First World War, 1918.

(who, incidentally, insists that it is 'English', not 'British'), this peculiar construct is scarcely even foreshadowed in eighteenth-century literature. But the nineteenth century is full of it. It springs into view, with two bounds, in 1814 in Jane Austen's *Mansfield Park* and then in 1816 in *Headlong Hall*, the masterpiece of Thomas Love Peacock, a food-lover who was also a writer of philosophical dialogues that he imagined to be novels.

The sad breakfast in *Mansfield Park* and the first meal in *Headlong Hall* have, let us say, small intimations of Greatness. In *Mansfield Park* Fanny Price is left to cry over two departures, and her tears are shed (equally or not) over the 'cold pork bones and mustard in William's plate' and the broken eggshells in Mr Crawford's. At this breakfast there were two relishes beyond the bread and butter.

The early scene in *Headlong Hall* is set in the breakfast room of an inn. The temporary hero, injured, 'contrived to be seated as near the fire as was consistent with his other object of having a perfect command of the table and its apparatus; which consisted not only of the ordinary comforts of tea and toast, but of a delicious supply of newlaid eggs, and a magnificent round of beef. Butter may be assumed alongside the toast, but again there are two further relishes, eggs and cold beef.

A little later in *Headlong Hall* comes the real revelation, the loving description of Squire Headlong's breakfast routine: 'It was an old custom in Headlong Hall to have breakfast ready at eight, and continue it till two; that the various guests might rise at their own hour, breakfast when they came down, and employ the morning as they thought proper.' A breakfast served from eight to two is an exaggeration, but it has a real basis, and its basis is not any single meal. It is a conflation of breakfast and the old midday dinner. At Headlong Hall, and among Peacock's contemporaries, dinner, formerly taken at midday, had been postponed to the evening. Peacock is the crucial informant here. His six-hour repast shows us that the Great nineteenth-century breakfast, described by so many of his successors, had a double origin, the old bread-and-butter breakfast and the old midday meal:

> During the whole of this period, the little butler stood sentinel at a side-table near the fire, copiously furnished with all the apparatus of tea, coffee, chocolate, milk, cream, eggs, rolls, toast, muffins, bread, butter, potted beef, cold fowl and partridge, ham, tongue, and anchovy. The Reverend Doctor Gaster found himself rather queasy in the morning, therefore preferred breakfasting in bed, on a mug of buttered ale and an anchovy toast.

It is just such a breakfast, though with more extravagant detail, that is demanded by the Revd Dr Folliott in Peacock's novel *Crotchet Castle*, published fifteen years after *Headlong Hall*: 'The divine took his seat at the breakfast-table, and began to compose his spirits by the gentle sedative of a large cup of tea, the demulcent of a well-buttered muffin, and the tonic of a small lobster.' Having reached that point, he speaks:

> The Rev. Dr Folliott: Chocolate, coffee, tea, cream, eggs, ham, tongue, cold fowl, – all these are good, and bespeak good

knowledge in him who sets them forth: but the touchstone is fish: anchovy is the first step, prawns and shrimps the second; and I laud him who reaches even to these: potted char and lampreys are the third, and a fine stretch of progression; but lobster is, indeed, matter for a May morning, and demands a rare combination of knowledge and virtue in him who sets it forth.

Mr Mac Quedy: Well, sir, and what say you to a fine fresh trout, hot and dry, in a napkin? or a herring out of the water into the frying pan, on the shore of Loch Fyne?

The Rev. Dr Folliott: Sir, I say every nation has some eximious virtue; and your country is pre-eminent in the glory of fish for breakfast. We have much to learn from you in that line at any rate.

A simpler approach to the big breakfast emerges in R. S. Surtees's stories. It's surely possible that Surtees read *Crotchet Castle* and was responding to it in his own boisterous and inimitable way when he wrote 'A Hunt Breakfast with Jorrocks', published just two years later in 1833:

It was a nice comfortable-looking place, with a blazing fire, half the floor covered with an old oil-cloth, and the rest exhibiting the cheerless aspect of the naked flags. About a yard and a half from the fire was placed the breakfast table; in the centre stood a magnificent uncut ham, with a great quartern loaf on one side and a huge Bologna sausage on the other; besides these there were nine eggs, two pyramids of muffins, a great deal of toast, a dozen ship-biscuits, and half a pork-pie, while a dozen kidneys were spluttering on a spit before the fire, and Betsey held a gridiron covered with mutton-chops on the top; altogether there was as much as would have served ten people.

'Now, sit down,' said Jorrocks, 'and let us be doing, for I am as hungry as a hunter. Hope you are peckish too; what shall I give you? tea or coffee? – but take both – coffee first and tea after a bit. If I can't give you them good don't know who can.

TRUE HUMILITY.

Right Reverend Host. "I'M AFRAID YOU'VE GOT A BAD EGG, MR. JONES!"
The Curate. "OH NO, MY LORD, I ASSURE YOU! PARTS OF IT ARE EXCELLENT!"

George du Maurier, 'The Curate's Egg', cartoon from *Punch*, 9 November 1895.

> You must pay your devours, as we say in France, to the am,
> for it is an especial fine one, and do take a few eggs with it;
> there, I've not given you above a pound of am, but you can
> come again, you know – waste not want not. Now take some
> muffins, do, pray. Betsey, bring some more cream, and set
> the kidneys on the table, the learned editor is getting nothing
> to eat. Have a chop with your kidney . . .'

A quartern-loaf, incidentally, is a four-pound loaf – a very big one.
Later editions of this text insert an apostrophe before the 'am'.

Leaping forwards 65 years and turning from fiction to something
approximating fact, we can appeal for further insight on the Great
breakfast to the mid-Edwardian edition of Mrs Beeton quoted above.
Here are the two suggested 'breakfast menus for a large party – winter'
in the *Book of Household Management* of 1907: 'Toasted wheat biscuits,
Omelettes fines herbes, Fried eggs (beurre noir), Coquille of turbot,
Grilled steak, Cold ham, Potted shrimps, Apples and bananas, Scones,
rolls, toast, bread, butter, marmalade, jam, tea, coffee, cream, milk' or,
'Cream of wheat, Fish omelet, Poached eggs on toast, Fillets of sole à

l'Horly, Stewed kidneys, Grilled bacon, Cold game, Cold ham, Stewed figs and cream, Scones, rolls, toast, bread, butter, marmalade, jam, tea, coffee, cream, milk.'

As we evaluate the truth and goodness of this Great breakfast tradition it is impossible to omit – and impossible to forget – 'the well-furnished breakfast-parlour at Plumstead Episcopi' imagined, about twenty years after *Headlong Hall*, by Anthony Trollope in *The Warden* for his henpecked hero Archdeacon Grantly:

> The tea consumed was the very best, the coffee the very blackest, the cream the very thickest; there was dry toast and buttered toast, muffins and crumpets; hot bread and cold bread, white bread and brown bread, home-made bread and bakers' bread, wheaten bread and oaten bread; and if there be other breads than these, they were there; there were eggs in napkins, and crispy bits of bacon under silver covers; and there were little fishes in a little box, and devilled kidneys frizzling on a hot-water dish; which, by the bye, were placed closely contiguous to the plate of the worthy archdeacon himself. Over and above this, on a snow-white napkin, spread upon the sideboard, was a huge ham and a huge sirloin; the latter having laden the dinner table on the previous evening. Such was the ordinary fare at Plumstead Episcopi.

The subtlety of Trollope is such that in savouring this passage out of context the reader will scarcely credit that there can be anything wrong with the breakfast-parlour at Plumstead Episcopi. Has the author allowed his ante-prandial enthusiasm to run away with him? Far from it. The meal is assiduously framed in gloom and negativity, the silver as if chosen 'to spend money without obtaining brilliancy or splendour', the room with its 'air of heaviness' and the whole house 'somewhat dull' and 'never . . . pleasant'. Trollope's Great breakfast is typical – the sirloin correctly left over from the previous day's dinner, everything else profuse and fresh and perfect all the way to the devilled kidneys – and beyond all reason. Trollope doesn't like it, any more than Hermann, Prince von Pückler-Muskau, on his tour of British-ruled Ireland in

1828, liked the breakfasts – breakfasts very much in the Surtees style – that he found there:

> I was on horseback by six o'clock, on my way to breakfast at Captain S–'s country-house, where the sportsmen were to rendezvous for a hare-hunt. I found six or seven sturdy squires assembled . . . After we had eaten and drunk the most hetero-geneous things – coffee, tea, whisky, wine, eggs, beef-steaks, honey, mutton-kidneys, cakes, and bread and butter, one after another – the company seated themselves on two large cars, and took the direction of the Galtee mountains.

Such are the novelistic and real breakfasts of nineteenth-century country houses, as well as certain other environments that resemble big country houses in being somewhat detached from ordinary life. Jesus College, Cambridge, for example: 'What a breakfast we had! . . . "Oh! you want coffee do you?" and away flew Mullins and brought down some-one else's big coffee pot.' At this breakfast, recalled by Mary Howitt, 'ample justice' was done 'to the pickled salmon, ducks, fowls, tongue, and pigeon-pie'. At Eton College, as remembered without fondness by Edward Spencer Mott, the 'inferior youths', 'hereditary bondsmen' and 'lower boys' (he was one of these before his well-deserved expulsion at fifteen) served their 'lords and masters' with a similarly elaborate breakfast.

Early twentieth-century parental breakfasts are similarly recalled with a frisson of horror by children who had to eat according to separate rules. Nancy Mitford in 1962 remembered 'whiffs of fried bacon from my father's breakfast and the sight of him tucking into sausage rolls or sausage mash, cold gammon and cranberry sauce, pork chops with apple sauce, pigs' thinkers and trotters and Bath chaps were daily tortures'. For the Mitford sisters the rules had been different for their parents not only because adults always ate as much as they liked of whatever they liked but also because their mother wouldn't allow the children to eat pork. 'Pigs' thinkers' are brains, it seems. Was her father eating all those things every day, or on some arcane weekly timetable? It's too late to ask.

Arnold Palmer in *Movable Feasts* was perhaps the first to outline the rise and fall of this big breakfast tradition: he glimpsed its beginnings

Ferdinand Max Bredt, *Frühstück zu Kriegszeiten*, 1918, oil on canvas.
'Breakfast in wartime': no men.

in the early nineteenth century, and he wrote with gloomy conviction that by 1952, so many other things in Britain having recently gone wrong, the big breakfast, also, was a thing of the past. He treats it as a purely insular development, as does O'Connor in *The English Breakfast*. However, looking back across the Channel, during the very same period when Thomas Love Peacock first described a recognizably Great breakfast, Grimod de la Reynière was chronicling similar changes in Parisian breakfasting and lunching habits.

I have always wondered whether the Great breakfast might have a longer pedigree. Could it have been introduced, far earlier, initially to the royal court alone, when James I arrived from Scotland to take his rightful place at the Palace of Westminster in 1603? The first in the long series of royal household ordinances that hints at this particular extravagance is the *Establishment of Prince Henry* laid down in 1610. Henry, James's son and heir, was fated to die in 1612, the succession passing to his younger brother Charles.

For the Prince his highnes breakefast:

manchet	2
cheate fine	2
cheate	4
beere	3 gallons
wine	1 picher
beefe	1 service
mutton	1 service
chickennes	2

Two kinds of bread had been the normal provision for royal tables – here we have three. Ale or wine had been the normal beverage – Prince Henry has both beer and wine (beer, technically, differing from ale in being flavoured with hops). Cold beef was the normal relish – Prince Henry and his breakfast attendance have beef, mutton and a couple of chickens. Yet James in his own household ordinances, laid down in 1604, had repeated to the point of dullness his intention to avoid

Gustave Courbet, *The Hunt Breakfast*, 1858, oil on canvas.

increasing the expenditure recorded for Elizabeth's court and wherever possible to reduce it. It did not take long for these good intentions to go by the wayside in regulating the establishment of his eldest son.

If the fashion for big breakfasts was introduced by royalty at this period it would eventually have filtered downwards to less royal break-fasters, if only for special occasions. Samuel Pepys once, at least, offered a breakfast of remarkable extravagance to a family party. This was on 1 January 1661, a doubly special day – his first opportunity to celebrate New Year since the restoration of the monarchy:

> Comes in my Brother Tho., and after him my father, Dr Tho. Pepys, my uncle Fenner and his two sons . . . to breakfast. I have for them a barrel of oysters, a dish of neat's tongues, and a dish of anchoves – wine of all sorts, and Northdown ale.

Pepys as host will have wanted to do things well on this occasion, to please not only his father but also his elder brother Thomas, not to mention his cousin, the unpleasant Thomas, who is a doctor, and three relatives by marriage, the Fenners. All the individual items in Pepys's New Year breakfast menu can easily be paralleled in others. It is the number of relishes – three of them, all special and costly – and the fact that there are at least three kinds of wine as well as ale, that make this breakfast unique both in Pepys's diary and in the contemporary record.

To reinforce the hypothesis that the Great breakfast was introduced from Scotland to England under Stuart influence it would be necessary to show that the Great Scottish breakfast was even older, at the royal Stuart court if nowhere else. But this I cannot do. The oldest detailed descriptions of Scottish breakfasts place them very close to Greatness, but they are nowhere near as old as James VI and I. Samuel Johnson's Hebridean breakfast in *Journey to the Western Islands of Scotland* is a landmark here.

> A man of the Hebrides, for of the women's diet I can give no account, as soon as he appears in the morning, swallows a glass of whisky; yet they are not a drunken race, at least I never

was present at much intemperance; but no man is so abstemious as to refuse the morning dram, which they call a skalk . . .
Not long after the dram, may be expected the breakfast, a
meal in which the Scots, whether of the lowlands or mountains, must be confessed to excel us. The tea and coffee are
accompanied not only with butter, but with honey, conserves,
and marmalades. If an epicure could remove by a wish, in quest
of sensual gratification, wherever he had supped he would
breakfast in Scotland.

We notice first of all that Hebrideans (Johnson is not speaking of
all Scotsmen) had the habit, on first rising, of a preliminary breakfast
which was not so very different from the traditional Mediterranean
'mouth-cleansing' – granting the absence of bread and the substitution
of whisky for wine. The main breakfast followed later, and this, as
Johnson experienced it, was a revelation to him. The description is an
additional confirmation that Johnson's own English breakfast at this
fairly prosperous period in his life (tea and rolls and butter according
to his chronicler Boswell) was the typical English breakfast in his time:
if it had been otherwise Johnson could hardly have expected his readers
to believe him when he claimed that wherever an epicure might be at
supper time, he would choose, given the power of instantaneous travel,
to be in Scotland at breakfast time.

Walter Scott in *Waverley*, set in 1746 during the aftermath of the
Jacobite rebellion but published in the same year as *Mansfield Park*
(1814), has Johnson's observations in mind. Scott, however, sits his
English traveller down to a much heavier Scottish breakfast.

[Waverley] found Miss Bradwardine presiding over the tea
and coffee, the table loaded with warm bread, both of flour,
oatmeal, and barleymeal, in the shape of loaves, cakes, biscuits,
and other varieties, together with eggs, reindeer ham, mutton
and beef ditto, smoked salmon, marmalade, and all the other
delicacies which induced even Johnson himself to extol the
luxury of a Scotch breakfast above that of all other countries.
A mess of oatmeal porridge, flanked by a silver jug, which held

an equal mixture of cream and butter-milk, was placed for the
Baron's share of this repast.

This fictional table, complete with literary reference to Johnson, is
laden with three kinds of bread, eggs, three kinds of salt meat, smoked
salmon and much else. There is a choice of tea or coffee, rare indeed in
eighteenth-century breakfasts, but reminiscent of the choice between
wine and beer at Prince Henry's breakfasts. Waverley's host, who has not
yet put in an appearance, will evidently be expecting porridge and will
lace it with 'an equal mixture of cream and butter-milk'. As we shall
observe later, the unlucky Waverley is not in the ideal frame of mind to
do justice to this lavish repast. It was more fully appreciated by Scott's
readers, including Hermann von Pückler-Muskau, who stayed in the
1820s at the inn at Llangollen in North Wales and breakfasted on

> smoking coffee, fresh Guinea-fowls' eggs, deep yellow moun-
> tain butter, thick cream, toasted muffins (a delicate sort of
> cake eaten hot with butter), and lastly, two red spotted trout
> just caught . . . a breakfast which Walter Scott's heroes in the
> highlands might have been thankful to receive.

The breakfasts observed by Johnson and imagined by Scott tend
towards luxury. Scott nonetheless includes – though Johnson omits –
the one constituent that most people think of as essential to a Scottish, and
indeed an Irish breakfast: 'See that hale old gentleman in the coffee-room
of an hotel at Dublin or Edinburgh,' wrote Thomas Forester in 1850.

> While yonder effeminate loungers are indulging in buttered
> muffins . . . the waiter sets before him a plate of his national
> mess, without which his morning meal would be incomplete.
> Which, think you, best preserves his constitution unimpaired,
> and may hope to enjoy a vigorous old age?

The answer – 'his national mess' – is porridge (or, as the Irish
called it, stir-about) and Forester's meticulous recipe will be quoted
in chapter Three.

From Scott onwards the gastronomic reputation of the Celtic fringe flourished in southeastern Britain, lasting through the generations into a period when London breakfasts had begun to take on flavours that were not so much Scottish as Imperial. Conan Doyle confirms it in 'The Naval Treaty', a Sherlock Holmes story published in 1893: '"Mrs Hudson has risen to the occasion," said Holmes, uncovering a dish of curried chicken. "Her cuisine is a trifle limited, but she has as good an idea of breakfast as a Scotchwoman. What have you there, Watson?"' Watson finds ham and eggs, canonically English, and curried chicken – something very different again. That detail betrays the influence on the homeland of the nineteenth-century breakfasts of British India – and these are narrated in a long series of memoirs of colonial officers and their families.

We can pick up the flavour from Richard Burton's first book, *Goa and the Blue Mountains*, published in 1851. Burton has fled Goa for the cooler hills, the 'Neilgherries' as Englishmen used to spell them. This breakfast, like so many, is taken after an early morning journey. Like so many, it follows a drink (by 'discussing' Burton means 'imbibing'):

> A horse-keeper rising grumbling from his morning slumbers, comes forward to hold your nag, and, whilst you are discussing a cup of tea in the verandah, parades the animal slowly up and down before you . . . Presently the 'butler' informs you that your breakfast, a spatchcock, or a curry with eggs, and a plateful of unleavened wafers, called aps – bread being unprocurable hereabouts – is awaiting you. You find a few guavas or plantains, intended to act as butter . . .

Burton has a tantrum about the butter and there is no need to quote him further on that topic. This short quotation usefully supports a general principle, however: anything that helps the bread to go down is a relish. If there is butter, butter is among the relishes and it is only in that light that guava and plantain can be looked on as an alternative to butter which, most people would agree, they resemble in no other way.

We can compare this mid-nineteenth-century traveller's breakfast in southern India with the almost precisely contemporary memories of the philologist John Beames. His recorded breakfasts begin in 1856 when he was a student at Haileybury, near Hertford, preparing for a lifetime in the Indian Civil Service: 'our breakfast consisting of tea or coffee, excellent bread-and-butter, and . . . a mutton-chop or a curried sole or something of the kind'. So we have a selection of relishes but just one (besides butter) on each occasion. This collegiate lifestyle helped prepare an enthusiastic Haileybury novice for his first bachelor years in India. The boarding-house where Beames fetched up in Calcutta offered a fully Imperial breakfast at nine every morning. This followed (as we are by now not surprised to learn) an early cup of tea and a brisk ride.

> We usually got up between five or six in the morning and sat
> in our sleeping jackets and pyjamas on the veranda having tea
> . . . Breakfast . . . was rather an elaborate meal consisting of fish,
> mutton chops, cutlets or other dishes of meat, curry and rice,
> bread and jam and lots of fruit – oranges, plantains, lichis, pine-
> apples, papitas, or pummeloes – according to season. Some
> drank tea but most of us had iced claret and water.

Claret, incidentally, was the only item on this menu that was not covered in the monthly rate of 300 rupees (£30) for full board and lodging at Miss Wright's, 3 Middleton Street, Calcutta.

This is the kind of breakfast that is deserved only after exercise: those who get up late eventually regret it. Crabbe, the inactive educationalist, finds it difficult to face such a breakfast in Anthony Burgess's fictional trilogy of the last years of the British in Malaya. This is 100 years after Burton's and Beames's experiences, and the mixture has become a little more British. Crabbe's 'Pantagruelian breakfast', prepared by his Chinese servant Ah Wing, reflects a Malayan stereotype of what a colonial officer ought to consume: 'grapefruit, iced papaya, porridge, kippers, eggs and bacon with sausages and a mutton chop, and toast and honey'.

British-style breakfasts were exported in the nineteenth century not only to India and Malaya but also to the dominions, New Zealand, Australia and Canada. Notice the description of an early twentieth-century Australian breakfast in Henry Handel Richardson's *The Way Home*, from which more will be quoted in chapter Five: 'they had to eat

u.s. President George W. Bush holds a breakfast meeting with Congressional leaders, October 2001.

their way through chops and steaks, eggs and rissoles, barracouta and garfish, fruit, hot rolls, preserves, tea and coffee'.

As for the United States, the relishes of Oklahoma described by John Steinbeck – ham and 'gravy' – are repeated and clarified in Marjorie Kinnan Rawlings's memoir of early twentieth-century hammy Florida breakfasts:

> White bacon is cooked everywhere in about the same fashion. It is usually soaked a little while in warm water or in milk, squeezed dry, dipped in flour and fried to a crisp golden brown. The large amount of grease that fries from it is poured into a bowl and this to the backwoods-man is 'gravy'. It is solid grease, and it is poured over grits, over sweet potatoes, over cornbread or soda biscuits.

The familiar ham and eggs (and the ubiquitous gravy) still appear today. They are prominent in the Chinese-owned café of Frank Chin's novel *Donald Duk* (1991), as the manager lays out hot breakfasts: 'You hammaneck over ease, sticky potatoes . . . Beckon anna scramboo, ricce no grave . . . Pork chop, poachecks, Frenchie fries, you. Sausage patties, sunnyside ups. Okay. You a waffoo. I get the syrup, don't worry.'

Scrambled eggs, poached eggs, fried eggs sunny side up are all canonical, but potatoes, waffles and maple syrup are foreign to British breakfast tradition. The u.s. has introduced other alien species alongside these. '"You wan' some breakfast, sugah?" "How about a couple of hard poached eggs, toast, and grits?" "Wheat or white?" "Wheat." . . . I smushed the eggs into the grits and mixed in a little butter and ate it between bits of the toast', says the heroic private eye in Robert Crais's crime novel *Voodoo River*, finding himself at a hot food stall somewhere in the Deep South. So grits may be 'wheat' or 'white'? British travellers would have been out of their depth, but Elvis Cole is ready to smash his poached eggs into his wheatmeal porridge and knows exactly what to do with the butter.

If these u.s. examples seem rather downmarket when viewed as analogues of the Great British breakfast of the Victorian period, they are not the full picture. Really extensive breakfasts were prescribed for the most fashionable early twentieth-century Americans by their advisers. One of these, Paul Pierce, suggested breakfasts and teas in a book of that title in 1907. Pierce's five-course 'chrysanthemum breakfast' is among his lighter meals. Chicken, once offered all on its own by the Countess of Montferrat to the lubricious King of France, is in good company here:

The time ten o'clock . . . Have three schemes of color for decorations – white chrysanthemums for parlor, pink for library, and yellow for dining-room. Serve at small tables, with rich floral center pieces, and handsomely draped with Battenburg or linen center piece and plate tumbler doylies.

FIRST COURSE: A small cluster of grapes served on dessert plates
SECOND COURSE: Baked apple (remove the core and fill with cooked oatmeal [!]; bake and serve with whipped cream over the whole)
THIRD COURSE: Chicken croquettes, scalloped potatoes, buttered rolls, celery, coffee

Eggs Benedict: English muffins halved and topped with ham, poached eggs and hollandaise sauce. As with some other named recipes, it's not clear which Benedict invented the dish.

Vegemite, an Australian invention of 1921, initially to fill the yawning gap created by a temporary shortage of British Marmite.

FOURTH COURSE: Fruit and nut salad, served in small cups on a bread and butter plate, with a wafer
FIFTH COURSE: Ice cream, in chocolate, pink and white layers; angel food, and pink and white layer cake

'Have a dish of salted almonds on each table', Pierce advises finally. His recommendation for a 'noonday breakfast' or, to express it more enticingly, 'a very swell breakfast for a swagger set' is, like some of Grimod de la Reynière's, too heavy for extensive quotation here, but the drinks, by themselves, are enough to establish the tone. 'Tea is not on the regulation breakfast list,' he points out, 'but of course it may be served if it is desired. Cider, malt liquors, the lighter wines, and in summer the various "cups" or fruit punches are in order; the breakfast wines are sherry, hock or Rhine wine, sauterne and champagne.'

Mrs François Berger Moran arrives for breakfast with Mrs Woodrow Wilson, 1913.

Constituents of a traditional Japanese breakfast, here laid out in all their elegant variety.

three

Breakfast
Across Space

> Breakfast foods are thought to be typically eaten during morning hours, these foods are distinct from other foods even if eaten outside of the morning. In this sense, some serve breakfast for supper.
>
> Wikipedia, 'Breakfast' (2011)

There is obvious good sense to be found in those two sentences. We've seen the ways in which breakfast foods 'are distinct from other foods', and we won't argue with people who think that breakfast foods are 'eaten during morning hours'. Also apparent in this quotation is the chronic indecision that makes it such a challenge to extract truth from the encyclopaedia that anyone can edit. There is no need to make any concession to the insomniac and confused Wikipedians who get themselves breakfast 'outside of the morning'. In the following geographical survey, as elsewhere in this book, breakfast is the first meal of the day, it is never the largest meal and, I firmly insist, it is taken before noon.

The Leftovers

We identified two contributing resources in the creation of breakfast, both of which arise from practices that Neolithic peoples were the first to adopt. Breakfast feeds the hungry, hard-working human with food that is easy and quick to assemble because it is (a) kept in long-term storage or (b) left over from yesterday's dinner.

This second resource, mentioned in our first literary breakfast –
Eumaios served 'roast meat that had been left uneaten the day before'
– is nowadays not so prominent in breakfast habits. South and East Asia
are the main regions of the modern world where breakfasting on leftovers is normal, and there are good reasons for this. Rice is the usual
cereal staple. Once it has been prepared for a main meal, rice comes to
no harm if kept overnight and is easy to reheat. The result is good to eat
and nourishing. On the other hand, given both heat and humidity, storage is more difficult in this part of the world than in most others: it is
wise to use up any leftovers before the temperature rises.

Thus in Japan, Vietnam, Burma and several other neighbouring
countries people are likely to use leftover items from yesterday's dinner
in today's breakfast. The rice is often combined with other foods during
the re-cooking process; it is frequently fried (having previously been
boiled), sometimes with added spices; it may be formed into thin cakes
or biscuits. In all these ways its look, texture and flavour will be different
from that of the previous day's boiled rice. If there's no rice left over, the
time needed to prepare more is still manageable. If there are no relishes
left over, but rice alone, then small quantities of a strongly flavoured
relish can be added to the rice without any trouble. In Indonesia, for
example, it takes very little *ikan teri* (salted dried anchovy) to excite the
morning taste buds; or, less startling to the European palate, a fried egg
might be the choice.

In the Philippines the leftover habit has sparked the creation of a
whole genre of breakfast dishes, all of them based on *si nangag*, which
is rice, first boiled (in origin, boiled for yesterday's dinner), then freshly
fried with salt and cloves of garlic. The *si nangag* is combined with
fried or scrambled egg (*itlog*) and with at least one meaty ingredient in
small quantity. Commonly this third ingredient is *tapa*, thinly sliced
meat cured with salt and spices to preserve it. The *tapa* is briefly fried
or grilled before it joins the rice and egg. This classic combination is
known under the portmanteau term *tapsilog*. The range of alternatives
now offered by breakfast restaurants in the Philippines includes a whole
series of portmanteau words: *tocilog* made with *tocino*, fried lightly
cured bacon also familiar in the Caribbean; *longsilog* made with a spicy
smoked sausage, *longganisa*, an ancient Mediterranean delicacy that

takes new forms in the Philippines; *litsilog* made with sucking pig (*lechón* in Spanish), roasted until the skin is crisp; *adosilog* made with meat long marinated in vinegar, garlic and soy sauce, then fried in oil. This *adobo*, named after a Spanish stew, has turned into something very different in Philippine cuisine: owing to its vinegar content it keeps well and tastes astonishing.

There are good reasons why using up leftovers has become less prevalent today as a source for breakfast. 'Would ye both eat your cake and have your cake?', they used to say in the sixteenth century, and 'You can't have your cake if you eat it' in the nineteenth, and they meant quite precisely this: if you eat it at dinner you can't have it for breakfast. Aside from that, long-term food storage at home is easier than it used to be; foods that are designed to keep are easier to buy, in greater variety, than they once were. In most parts of the world such foods can now easily constitute a quickly prepared breakfast. Hence, if there are leftovers, they are frugally re-used at lunch instead; less frugally, fed to household pets and pigs; or, even less frugally, discarded.

The One-dish Breakfast

A breakfast in a single dish is likely to have been the daily norm once upon a time, at least in regions where the typical breakfast foods require a dish at all. Bowls were once rare, costly and not to be lightly multiplied. A single-dish breakfast is now also something of a regional trait, and applies to the same broad region mentioned above – South and East Asia.

Noodle soup is the usual basis, being quicker to prepare and easier to handle than a dish in which the same soup is added to rice. In Japan and Korea and across eastern and southern China the same type of breakfast is many people's daily choice; in the nineteenth and twentieth centuries, with the Chinese diaspora, it spread more widely, to the Philippines, Indonesia and Malaysia, Vietnam, Cambodia, Laos, Thailand and Burma. The soup is more or less clear; its basis may be fish or chicken or meat stock; its additional contents are typically herbs, more or less spicy; the noodles are the cereal element that every breakfaster across the world expects.

Rice noodles for breakfast, Guilin, China.

The Japanese version is *misoshiru*, a soup whose liquid basis is *dashi*, stock made with seaweed (specifically kelp, *Saccharina japonica*) or shiitake mushrooms. This is already nourishing and tasty: it was in *dashi* kelp stock that the 'fifth flavour', *umami*, was first identified a century ago. To this stock is added *miso*, a salty, strongly flavoured and highly nourishing product of soya beans or rice fermented by means of the mould *Aspergillus oryzae*, which also effects the fermentation of sake, and whose history in Japan goes back as much as 2,000 years.

Mohinga is the national breakfast in Burmese towns and cities, certainly for those who eat on the way to work. This is a recent development, spreading from the great big civilization in the east like many other features of modern Burmese cuisine, yet assuming a highly individual local form. For the last half century *mohinga* has grown steadily in popularity, and instant packet versions are sold to those who can't do without it even at home. This dish of rice vermicelli in fish broth is always available at street stalls: to it is added chickpea flour or toasted rice, lemon grass, onions, garlic, ginger, pepper and powerfully flavoured *ngapi* (fish paste), and it is served with fried onions, dried chilli, fresh green coriander – the unmistakable and ubiquitous aroma of Burmese cuisine – and fish sauce. A version originating in Arakan (northwestern Burma) and increasingly familiar elsewhere is flavoured with snakefish flakes, chilli paste and other fiery spices, as its nickname *ah pu shar pu* – 'burn throat burn tongue' – suggests.

Noodle soups made for breakfast in the Philippines include *batchoy*, based on chicken stock to which pork offal and pork crackling is added. Circumstantial stories are told of its invention and naming (in La Paz market, Iloilo, in 1938, according to one story): the stories may well contain a degree of truth, but *batchoy* certainly emerged from the Chinese community of Panay and was evidently transferred, as a general idea if not a specific recipe, from coastal southern China from which this community largely migrated.

The noodle soups of Taiwan, southern China and Laos may qualify as one-dish breakfasts or they may not: they are often accompanied by *youtiao*, a double fried doughnut or breadstick. The *youtiao* has a long local history in Canton and a firmly embedded legendary origin. It represents the unlucky or wicked chancellor Qin Hui and his wife, popularly blamed for the death of good general Yue Fei in 1142. Their punishment for the last 850 years has been to be deep fried, torn apart, dipped in noodle soup and eaten by millions of Chinese every day. Under Chinese culinary influence noodle soups became popular in Vietnam in the early twentieth century (*phở*, a rice noodle soup with beef or chicken, is traced to the Hanoi region in the 1920s) but under French culinary influence French bread is dipped into them.

At least one other region of the world is notable for its breakfast soups, but they are very different in style. In the Peruvian mountains thick soups based on maize (hominy, in American terms) with the addition of offal are eaten; the people around Bogotá and in the Cundinamarca region of Colombia eat a milk and egg soup, *changua*, flavoured with salt and green coriander, garnished with spring onions and poured over stale leftover bread.

These soups are seldom entirely one-dish breakfasts because, liquid though they are, one of the typical breakfast drinks – typically tea – is likely to arrive alongside them. That is evidently true also of the one-dish solid breakfasts popular in some neighbouring regions. From southern Thailand across Malaysia, Singapore and Indonesia rice dishes in various forms not only serve for many people's breakfast but have attained the status of national dishes: *nasi lemak* – fat rice; *nasi dagang* – trade rice; *nasi goreng* – fried rice; and *nasi uduk* – mixed rice are only the best known of a long list. *Nasi lemak* is typical of the west coast of the Malay peninsula, *nasi dagang* the east coast, *nasi uduk* the islands. All three are based on rice cooked in coconut milk instead of water, with added aromatics: for *nasi uduk* cloves, cassia and lemon grass; for *nasi dagang* fenugreek seeds and sliced shallots; for *nasi lemak* pandanus leaves and sometimes ginger. Often wrapped in banana leaves, these dishes will have addenda such as egg or omelette, spicy chicken or beef, pickled vegetables, fried anchovies, fried onion; there is likely to be *sambal kacang* – peanut chilli paste. *Nasi dagang* is fishier, including a spicy tuna dish redolent of galangal, chilli, turmeric and lemon grass. Unlike the other three, *nasi goreng* is based on fried rice, and is often supposed to have been introduced from southern China in medieval times: it can certainly be seen as a typically Chinese means of using up already-cooked rice. In modern *nasi goreng* the fried rice will probably be flavoured with garlic, shallots, tamarind and chilli, may have egg or chicken or prawns on the side or, more simply, salted dried anchovy may be added as flavouring.

The Middle East has a very different one-dish breakfast: its name is *shakshuka*, a word whose meaning is stated more confidently than its etymology. The meaning is given as 'mixture', a safe bet, since that is unmistakably what it is: eggs poached in a sauce of tomatoes, chillis and onions, flavoured with cumin. Traditionally cooked and often served in a cast-iron pan, it requires bread to soak up the sauce. There is a Turkish equivalent, *menemen*, but with scrambled egg, sometimes olives, sometimes sausage or *pastırma* (dried beef). And there is a transatlantic reincarnation, *huevos rancheros*, familiar in Mexico and elsewhere: the eggs, this time, are fried; the bread becomes tortillas, whether maize or wheat; refried beans and avocado or guacamole may invade; but

Nasi goreng. A fried rice dish, the most traditional and popular of Indonesian and Malayan breakfasts.

the tomato and chilli sauce holds its place. There is finally a Yucatán variant, *huevos motuleños*, known also in Cuba, in which the eggs on tortillas remain but the tomatoes have given way at last – to black beans and cheese.

The Beverage

Whatever the lovers of coffee and chocolate may say, and whatever rearguard action may be fought by those who take wine, whisky or *sljivovica* for their breakfast, tea is the world's breakfast drink, an astonishing success for a weakly flavoured herbal infusion unknown outside eastern Asia until the sixteenth century.

Tea is surely native to the mountains of southwestern China, far from the original northern centres of Chinese power. It was known in the north, it is said, in the second century BC (much earlier, some say, but such assertions for the present are impossible to confirm). In Chinese literature far more feeling goes into the consideration of this beverage than into any other aspect of the morning meal, as in *The Story of the Stone* (or *Dream of the Red Chamber*), in which on one occasion the young Bao Yu suddenly recalls his breakfast tea:

> 'When you made that Fung Loo this morning,' he said to Snowpink, 'I remember telling you that with that particular brand the full flavour doesn't come out until after three or four waterings . . . This would have been just the time to have the Fung Loo.'
>
> 'I was keeping it for you,' said Snowpink, 'but Nannie Li came and drank it all.'

Bao Yu smashes his cup on the floor, where it shatters and splashes Snowpink's skirt with hot tea, a typical reaction that helps to define his spoilt character at this early point in the novel.

Tea continues to be the national drink, at breakfast as at other meals, taken as 'Chinese tea', very hot, light, as it comes (no milk and no sugar), in small cups frequently replenished from a teapot which is itself replenished if needed. In Japan, Korea and across Southeast Asia tea is by far the most popular breakfast drink, but in all these places coffee now invades too.

In Hong Kong (the British are to be blamed for this) many drink tea with milk. It is even enjoyed as a unique half tea, half coffee milky mix, *yuanyang*, a conjugal pairing as disparate as male and female Mandarin ducks (yes, it gets its name from the ducks).

There is home-grown tea, good tea, in Malaysia and Burma. Westwards from there Indian tea takes the place of Chinese in the breakfast cup. It is the national drink of Sri Lanka and of India itself, where some at breakfast prefer *masala chai*, mixture tea, infused with spices and herbs. In Pakistan, too, they take tea; in Afghanistan some like it with rose essence or cardamom seeds; in Iran and the Middle East generally it is taken in a different style, sweetened; westwards again, from Libya to Morocco, it will be mint tea, which is green tea in basis, much sweetened and aromatized with mint.

Tea, the legacy of Empire, retains its power in Britain. Some drink it without milk, perhaps choosing Earl Grey tea with a jasmine flavour, and adding a slice of lemon; but the vast majority add milk (disputing whether the milk or the tea goes first into the cup) and many add sugar too. People still drink tea wherever the Empire once reached, from Ireland via Nigeria and Uganda and Kenya (where much tea is grown) to Australia and New Zealand. Only in the United States, where in colonial days the duty on tea raised prices and hackles, did the tea habit give way to coffee. As for the British themselves, they are famous for their inability to make coffee properly, as the Swiss pastor Charles P. Moritz severely observed in 1782: 'I would always advise those who wish to drink coffee in England, to mention beforehand how many cups are to be made with half an ounce; or else the people will probably bring them a prodigious quantity of brown water.' If Moritz's opinion (and mine) are doubted, Arnold Palmer, who guided me to Moritz's travels, confirms it. 'From the days of Charles II to those of George II,' Palmer narrates, 'more coffee was bought and brewed by the Londoner than by any citizen in the world. There is no evidence that he ever learned or wished to learn the knack of making it, or knew that there was one. Repeated efforts to instruct him have left him almost unmoved.'

They discovered and grew it in Ethiopia; they spread it through the Islamic Near East to the Mediterranean; it is in Italy, to judge by the names of styles (*espresso*, *cappuccino*, *latte*, like movements of a sonata) that they really know how to make it. It is in the modern United States, and across much of the American continent, that they best know how to drink it. And nearly two-thirds of it is drunk at breakfast time. In most American countries, coffee is the majority breakfast beverage, sometimes in a local style such as the almost-Greek strong black coffee of Ecuador, *café de olla*, brewed in a small aluminium pot, or the sweet-and-salty *café con leche* of Cuba. Black coffee is so important to the Brazilian breakfast that it gives its name to the meal, *café-da-manhã*.

The taste for coffee is worldwide and is on the increase; someone fashionable is drinking it everywhere, hot and black, with sugar, with fresh milk and cream, with dried milk, with evaporated milk, chilled, on ice. The fact that it is ever more widely grown helps spread it further: local coffees are popular in local markets, such as the unusual *kape barako* of the Philippines. Local styles are numerous. In Vietnam they drink *cà phê sữa đá*, local dark and strong filter coffee with sweetened condensed milk, poured over ice. So important did this become to those who had lived in and left Vietnam that the flavour is now imitated, using chicory, in the u.s.

Chicory root, European in origin, is one of many coffee substitutes that became popular in countries where coffee was expensive or in short supply. These substitutes have sometimes seized new markets, in times when coffee is plentiful, as caffeine-free beverages, though it is difficult to say what they have in their favour to compensate for the caffeine they lack. So it is with chicory in Louisiana and with dandelion root elsewhere. So it was for a long time with Postum, made from wheat bran, molasses and other ingredients, proudly named in 1895 by its inventor C. W. Post. It was marketed to American mothers for their children, highly popular with adults, especially when coffee was rationed, but discontinued in 2007 to the distress of many. Variants made with barley still survive: Inka, a popular Polish breakfast drink, Caro, Pero and Barleycup.

The third of the trilogy of stimulating breakfast drinks which spread to new markets in the sixteenth and seventeenth centuries is chocolate. In this case the spread was not so spectacular. Hot chocolate, historically the stimulant of Aztec monarchs, is a beverage of choice in Colombia and through Central America and also in Spain and France. Elsewhere it has a minority following, sometimes as a drink for children who have not yet developed a tea or coffee habit. It is more nourishing and less addictive than the other two, with a taste that is more immediately attractive. The taste of cocoas, of Nesquik and Ovaltine, may be almost as enticing to some, while Cola Cao, a high-energy cocktail of chocolate and cola nut extract with added vitamins and minerals, has sold well to Spanish parents who want fat children. It is now developing a market in China.

In much of Spain a traditional breakfast eaten at cafes is *chocolate con churros*. That the *churros* have a family relationship, via Portuguese trade, with the *youtiao* of southern China seems possible but remains uncertain. At any rate *churros* are long, narrow, deep-fried bread sticks which can be eaten sugared or dribbled with chocolate sauce, but at

Postum advertisement, 1910. An early appeal to the parental obsession with healthy breakfasts for children – compounded in this case with nervousness about caffeine addiction.

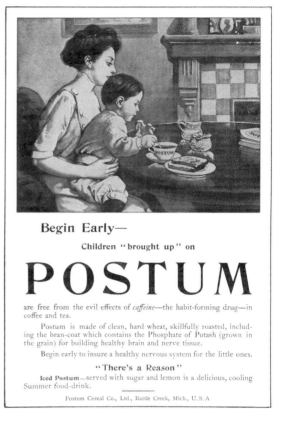

Begin Early—

Children " brought up " on

POSTUM

are free from the evil effects of *caffeine*—the habit-forming drug—in coffee and tea.

Postum is made of clean, hard wheat, skillfully roasted, including the bran-coat which contains the Phosphate of Potash (grown in the grain) for building healthy brain and nerve tissue.

Begin early to insure a healthy nervous system for the little ones.

" There's a Reason "

Iced Postum—served with sugar and lemon is a delicious, cooling Summer food-drink.

Postum Cereal Co., Ltd., Battle Creek, Mich., U. S. A

breakfast are typically dipped in hot drinking chocolate or in milky coffee. The *churros* are slightly salty; the chocolate is thick and sweet. There are of course equivalents elsewhere to this cafe breakfast – *cappuccino e brioche* in Italy, *café au lait* with a croissant in France.

From Iraq, Syria and Israel to Turkey, from Portugal to Spain and France, and then north across Europe from either direction, the mixture of breakfast beverages becomes inextricable. Coffee perhaps has an overall majority, but chocolate is favoured by some and tea by others, though very few drink it British fashion, with milk. Herbal infusions may replace tea; orange juice is popular; caffeine drinks like Coca-Cola are in demand. Milk on its own is the choice of some, is urged on children and was once a standard choice in *galaktopolia* 'milk shops' in Greece, though in that country it has now more or less given way to coffee in its various forms – from Greek coffee (very strong and sweetened) to *frappé* (iced, with milk). In general those who choose strong black coffee later in the day may prefer a big, nourishing cup of coffee with milk for breakfast.

We still have to survey the less widely drunk breakfast beverages. There is the stimulating *mate* of Argentina, *chimarrão* of Brazil, a tea-like infusion of the leaves of the *yerba mate* or *erva-maté* (*Ilex paraguariensis*), already prized, though not at breakfast, by Guaraní and Tupí peoples before the Europeans came. It is drunk very hot in small gourds. In the Andean countries, from Bolivia to Ecuador, there is a barley drink, *emoliente*, containing alfalfa, linseed and a local aromatic, *boldo* (*Peumus boldus*) which has something of bay about it and something of camphor. In Guatemala, Mexico and New Mexico there is *atol*, a thick drink based on maize flour or oatmeal, spiced with cinnamon, vanilla and sometimes chocolate.

Then there are the drinks based on milk, and typically sour or fermented milk since in pre-modern times only the lucky few could drink fresh milk when they wanted. In a very wide region of Russia, Eastern Europe and Central Asia there is *kefir* (one of various names) which is a briefly fermented, slightly alcoholic, health-giving soured milk. This can be made at home and is also widely sold with added flavourings, making it less sour. How the *kefir* habit reached Chile (where it is called *yogurt de pajaritos*, 'birds' yogurt') is not clear. In the Balkans, Turkey and Iraq, a little south of the *kefir* region, a different-tasting drink, *ayran*, made by mixing yogurt with salt and water, is a well-known beverage; very much alike is the *dugh* of Iran and the *lassi* of Pakistan, India and Bangladesh, which may be made sweet but is better salty. Soya milk, popular as a breakfast drink in China, Japan and Korea, is spreading further afield to meet the demand for a lactose-free milk substitute.

There is even a malted drink that has achieved international popularity on breakfast tables. Variously known as Malta, children's beer and wheat soda, it is brewed from barley and hops and is syrupy sweet and as brown as stout. In Latin America and the Caribbean it is drunk on ice and mixed with condensed or evaporated milk.

Gabriel Metsu, *Portrait of the Artist with his Wife, Isabella de Wolff, in a Tavern*, 1661, oil on canvas.

Alcoholic drinks (not counting the very lightly alcoholic *kefir*) are not as popular at breakfast as they were: depressant and intoxicating, alcohol has the wrong qualities for a morning beverage. In Serbia one would take a glass of *sljivovica*; in the Scottish Highlands, as we have seen, a nip of whisky. The champagne breakfast must be considered a rare luxury, occasionally tasted in Australia and New Zealand, but never in Champagne. In Denmark a bitters (the proudly named Gammel

Dansk, 'Old Danish') is enjoyed by a discerning clientele at breakfast, not daily but at weekends or on special occasions.

The Cereal

Breakfasts in southeastern China and in all the coastal regions of eastern Asia are based on rice. The two typical forms in which the rice is used are noodles, as discussed above, and congee – rice that has almost lost its texture after long boiling in plenty of water, becoming a kind of porridge. 'The first meal of the day was of soft rice, or *congee*,' wrote Mimie Ouei in *The Art of Chinese Cooking*. 'Dishes of salty or savoury foods . . . salted peanuts, salt vegetables and scrambled eggs, or as in my province of Fukien *jo sung*, a kind of mincemeat made of pork, were served with this gruel.' But congee stretches further. In Indonesia it is *bubur ayam* and may be accompanied by spring onion leaves, chicken and hot and sweet sauces. In southern India, too, from Andhra Pradesh to Karnataka, especially outside the cities, *kanji* (congee) is the basis of breakfast; it may be served with pickles, chutneys or the tamarind and lentil dish *sambar*. In Sri Lanka (where it is *arisi kanji* in Tamil, *kola kanda* in Sinhalese) green herbs, notably the ground-covering *gotu kola* (*Centella asiatica*), are added to it, and it may be made with milk (*pal kanji* in Tamil).

Maize porridge is the basis for breakfast in large parts of Africa. In South Africa it is *pap* (some might say it's pap everywhere, but in South Africa it's *called pap*); in Zimbabwe *sadza*; in Zambia and Malawi *nsima*; in East Africa *ugali*. The colour is white and the consistency varies – some is solid enough to be picked up in the hands and sticky enough to pick up flavour from them. In Ghana a roasted maize porridge, Tom Brown, is popular. But the *garri* of West Africa, often as solid as the *ugali* of the East, is made from cassava root, and has transferred to Brazil under the name of *farofa*.

The *bsisa* of Libya and other countries of North Africa is very different, a mixture of ground cereals (principally barley and wheat) combined with fenugreek, anise, cumin and sugar. It differs from the other congees and porridges not just in its contents, but in the fact that it is usually mixed with olive oil and eaten cold, with dried figs or dates,

'Natives at breakfast: movable chow shop.' Street food in Canton (Guangzhou), *c.* 1919.

as a quick meal. This is particularly useful to the nomadic Berber peoples of the Sahara and to other travellers, who can carry it with them dry and need only a little oil to make it edible.

Buckwheat porridge, *kasha*, is typical to Russian and Eastern European breakfasts, competing with wheatmeal and others. Wheatmeal porridge is well known in North America under such names as Cream of Wheat and Malt-O-Meal. There, however, it has two other competitors: in the south, hominy grits, the name for a local kind of maize meal; and oatmeal, which in Britain and Ireland is known simply as porridge. Grits is an authentic English name of which groats is the original form. Hominy, on the other hand, is borrowed from the Powhatan (Algonquian) word *utketchaumun*, 'that which is ground' – providing evidence of how maize was used. Hominy grits originate in eastern North America, the region of origin of maize itself, and it was from Native Americans that European settlers learned how to make them.

Oatmeal porridge is one of several delicacies (if that's the word) vying for the title of Scotland's national dish. Made with water or milk, eaten with salt, sugar, maple syrup or other flavour enhancers, it is popular across the northern hemisphere from Canada to Norway, Sweden, Latvia and Finland (where a favourite sweetener is lingonberry jam). The method used in nineteenth-century Norway is fully described in a travel narrative, Thomas Forester's *Norway in 1848 and 1849*, the aim being to explain the preparation of porridge to the benighted English reader (for a modern approach see the Recipes section).

> Take two or three handfulls of oatmeal, I prefer it of mixed coarse and fine meal, in the proportion of one-third of the latter to two of the former. At Vaagen and elsewhere in our rambles, we got rug-meel (rye-meal), and thought it an improvement. Mingle the meal in a basin of cold water and pour it into a saucepan containing about a quart of boiling water; add a small portion of salt. Set the saucepan over the fire, and keep stirring it (I have seen some of the Norwegian dames use a light whisk), sprinkling from time to time small quantities of the meal till the composition boils, and has acquired the proper consistency. That may be known by its glutinous state as it drops from the spoon. Let it simmer for ten minutes, and then pour it, not into a deep dish, but on common dinner plates, and it will form a soft, thin, jellied cake. Spoon out portions of this and float them in new milk, adding moist sugar to your taste.

Forester will be quoted again in chapter Five when he explains how effectively, if eaten with a slice of rye or wheat bread and an admixture of cream and sugar, this Norwegian oatmeal will fortify the hungry traveller who may have many miles to go before the next meal. But enough of congees and porridges.

Rice in its own right, boiled as grains that can still be recognized when they are served, is a common breakfast cereal too. Freshly boiled rice is familiar at breakfast in East and South Asia; it is the basis, for example, of the already-described one-dish breakfasts of Malaysia and Indonesia, *nasi goreng* and its relatives, where the 'one dish' may be a banana leaf. Otherwise, rice is the leftover that is typically refried. Another Indonesian breakfast is *lontong sayur*, compressed rice made by wrapping parboiled rice tightly in a banana leaf and boiling again. It can be served cold, sliced, with a spicy sauce, cooked vegetables and perhaps noodles, deep-fried peanuts and prawn crackers. *Ketupat*, a rice dumpling, is also popular.

Other sources of carbohydrate include the *tapioca* of northern Brazil, a manioc pancake filled with cheese, coconut and other things; the potatoes of pre-famine Ireland (as with rice, so with potatoes, frying makes palatable what was boiled for yesterday's dinner); and the *mangu* of the Dominican Republic, made from mashed ground plantain. These all have analogues elsewhere, though the breakfasts in Scene 2 of Thomas Pynchon's *Gravity's Rainbow* are more banana-stuffed than any real ones known to me. The fantasy encompasses 'banana omelets, banana sandwiches, banana casseroles . . . banana croissants and banana kreplach, and banana oatmeal and banana jam and banana bread' and much more.

In general, until the rise of 'breakfast cereals' whose story belongs to chapter Four, bread was the second great breakfast cereal. Wheat bread is far more widespread than breads made from rice, rye, maize or barley. In India and the Middle East flat (unleavened) breads serve the purpose. Less commonly, a deep-fried bread may be used, like the *youtiao* and *churros* already mentioned and the *luchi* of eastern India, made of fine white wheat flour (*maida* flour, often also used for nans) with a little ghee.

In northern and western China, in regions where rice does not constitute the typical breakfast cereal, bread takes its place. This bread may take many forms, baked or grilled, fried or steamed, flat or high-rise, maize or wheat. In his book *Princes of the Black Bone* (1959), Peter Goullart describes a breakfast in the hilly inland region of Sichuan:

The Szechuanese only had two meals during the day. One was at about ten o'clock in the morning and another roughly at about five in the afternoon. During breakfast, which was also called lunch, we had butter tea and momos with some salted turnips or cabbage and a little kanbar. Momos were lozenge-shaped baps made of roughly-milled Indian corn.

Goullart also travelled to more remote mountain-dwelling peoples, and in *Forgotten Kingdom* (1955) he describes breakfasts with an unexpected resemblance to those of central Europe – admittedly with differences too. At Xiaguan, among the Bai or Minchia, he 'breakfasted on native ham and cream cheese with *baba* (flat round bread enriched with butter and ham shavings), washed down with Tibetan butter tea'.

Europe is the epicentre of the idea of bread as the breakfast staple: for the poor of Europe it was for many centuries the whole of breakfast or almost the whole of it. In chapter Two, the quotation from Edmund

Ministers of the Regent at breakfast, 1938–9, Tibet.

Gosse's poem to an aromatic breakfast, 'The Poet at the Breakfast Table',
three lines were omitted:

> The loaves are beautiful and fair
> (As Wordsworth puts it), crust and crumb;
> The coffee hath an odour rare . . .

Gosse's poem gives a brief nod to Wordsworth (to whom 'waters on a
starry night are beautiful and fair') but in describing the bread, the focal
point of all English breakfasts in his time, Gosse looks back to a tradition rather than to any single author. He absorbs from that tradition all
the negative implications that the phrase 'crust and crumb' evokes and,
in a light poem, lightly turns them positive. As we shall see later, crust
and crumb ('the whole loaf' or 'the whole woman') is what the narrator
swears to renounce in Laurence Sterne's chapter of breakfasts (*The Life
and Opinions of Tristram Shandy*, Book 8 chapter 11), before his dear,
dear Jenny re-conquers him. The same phrase is used in Shakespeare's
King Lear by the King's fool in lines that may well be proverbial:

> He that keeps nor crust nor crumb,
> Weary of all, shall want some.

It is a direct warning to Lear, and of course a true prediction: nothing
(not even the means of making breakfast) will remain to one who is
unwise enough not to hold on to what he has.

From Europe, more recently, the most fashionable styles of bread
have been transferred to much of the rest of the world. In former French
colonies, from Morocco by way of Senegal to Vietnam, people are
familiar with long French loaves and baguettes, croissants and their
sweeter relatives – even if not everyone eats this way. British loaves and
ready-sliced bread are admired as breakfast fodder far beyond the
shores of the United Kingdom. Spain has transmitted the love of wheat
bread to its South American colonies, though in Mexico and Central
America it competes with maize-based breads such as *tortillas*,
empanadas or *arepas*. Argentina and Brazil are among the countries
that have drawn widely on European traditions; croissants and French

bread jostle with grilled sandwiches, crackers, *churros* and German pastries. Spongy British-style sandwich bread and flaky French-style croissants make a fashion statement in every big city alongside Italian-style roasted coffee.

British sliced bread goes back further in history than may be thought. Charles P. Moritz, quoted earlier on the subject of bad English coffee, has warm praise for the bread and toast that he took with a cup of tea for his breakfast:

> The fine wheaten bread, which I find here, besides excellent butter and Cheshire-cheese, makes up for my scanty dinners . . . The slices of bread and butter, which they give you with your tea, are as thin as poppy leaves. But there is another kind of bread and butter usually eaten with tea, which is toasted by the fire, and is incomparably good. You take one slice after the other and hold it to the fire on a fork until the butter is melted, so that it penetrates a number of slices at once: this is called *toast*.

Long a British and American favourite, toast gained new popularity at the beginning of the twentieth century with the invention of the electric toaster. The first really successful model appeared in 1909. Until then bread was toasted, with care and impatience, by holding it close to a naked flame; from then on it has been toasted, forgetfully and inconsistently, in a machine. In retrospect the decades from 1930 to 1960 are the toaster heyday. Some of the best machines from that golden age live on, still producing slices perfectly crisp on the outside and marrowy on the inside. When they die they go to heaven.

Sweeter forms of bread – *brioche* and *fouace* – have been popular in France and elsewhere. François Rabelais in *Gargantua*, narrating a fantasy war between the *fouaciers* of Lerné and the shepherds of the country round about (both close neighbours of the Rabelais family) explains very precisely the health benefits of these traditionally ember-baked sweet loaves when eaten with fresh fruit: 'Nota bene that all with constipated digestions will find grapes with fresh *fouaces* are a heavenly breakfast. They'll eject turds as long as a spear; they'll shit themselves when all they wanted was to fart.'

Worth a separate glance are the breakfast dishes, widespread across the world and very different from one another in detail, in which cereal foods are combined with pulses. Japan is a good place to begin, with *nattō*, soya beans fermented by the action of *Bacillus subtilis*. It is sometimes said to be a recent invention, on the grounds that there is no early historical record of its use, and sometimes traced back to hundreds of years bc, the argument being that the methods for its manufacture were available in Japan in the distant past. What is certain is that the current system of transferring a starter culture from one batch to the next was invented in the early twentieth century. The slippery texture of *nattō* is as strange as the smell (which has been compared to blue cheese) and taste. It is eaten with boiled rice.

Burma has its *htamin jaw*, fried rice with boiled peas, and its *kao hnyin baung*, sticky rice, steamed and wrapped in a banana leaf, with peas and a salty garnish of toasted sesame. In Burma Indian breads – nan, chapati and paratha – may also be served with peas, and in Orissa

A Burmese breakfast, *kao hnyin baung* – sticky rice with fried fish on a banana leaf.

mashed peas are among the fillings used in *luchi*, making up the dish *koraishutir kochuri*. A tradition in West Bengal is to eat semi-fermented rice (*panta bhath*) with dal or mashed lentils. Samosas, deep-fried pastry shells enclosing various fillings often featuring peas and lentils, are popular at breakfast not only in northwestern India, where they originate, but all around the Indian Ocean as far as South Africa; they have a distant resemblance to the *empanadas* popular in Spain and Latin America, though these are bigger, sometimes baked rather than fried and have different fillings.

If the Orissan *kochuri* mentioned above sounds familiar it is because it is brother or sister to the British *kedgeree*. I can do no better than to quote Henry Yule and Andrew Burnell (in *Hobson-Jobson*, 1903) on the origin and meaning of this name, which came to England straight from the heyday of the British Empire. Their nineteenth-century spelling is as savoury as their subject:

> Kedgeree or kitchery (Hindi *khichri*) a mess of rice, cooked with butter and dhall, and flavoured with a little spice, shred onion, and the like [query: what do they mean by 'the like'?]; a common dish all over India, and often served at Anglo-Indian breakfast tables . . . In England we find the word is often applied to a mess of re-cooked fish, served for breakfast, but this is inaccurate: fish is frequently eaten with kedgeree, but is no part of it.

Yule and Burnell point out that 'very old precedent is followed' when kedgeree is eaten for breakfast. The North African diplomat and Arabic author Ibn Battuta had already tasted *kishri* at breakfast on his visit to India around the year 1340 (he explained it as 'mung beans boiled with rice, buttered and eaten'). As for the fish, elsewhere in their dictionary Yule and Burnell repeat that the basic Indian *khichri* was a mixture of rice and beans or dal, and that the British in India often ate it this way but had also taken to adding fish, calling it 'fish kitcherie'. In Bombay the typical ingredient was the fish then known as bummelo: the modern name for it is Bombay duck (*Harpodon nehereus*). Incidentally the usual breakfast fish in British Calcutta at that time was a much larger creature,

Smoked haddock kedgeree.

the cockup, which for some reason has also changed its name and is known these days as barramundi (*Lates calcarifer*).

In appealing to a fourteenth-century traveller on the history of breakfast in India Yule and Burnell were well aware that they were not going to the fountainhead. Two full meals a day and two smaller meals were already canonical in classical Sanskrit texts a thousand years earlier, and the early small meal is certainly what we would call breakfast. What was eaten for a classical Indian breakfast is hard to specify, but rice and beans, or rice and cooked foods left over from the previous evening meal, are almost certain to have been the usual items on the menu.

In Egypt there are two breakfast dishes to list under this heading: first, *ful medames*, slow-cooked beans – and sometimes lentils – with an olive oil, lemon juice and garlic dressing; second, *falafel*. This, at least, is its international name, and it may well be Egyptian in origin, but its Egyptian name is different: *ṭa'miyya*. Long popular in northeast Africa and around the eastern Mediterranean, it consists of balls of ground bean or chickpea flour, often served and eaten in a wrapping of flat bread such as pita or *lafa*.

Many in West Africa eat breakfast dishes based on beans alone or beans plus cereals. In Ghana people buy *waakye* (rice cooked with beans) from street stalls. In northern Nigeria among the Hausa, *kosai* (fried cakes of black-eyed beans) alternate with *funkaso* (wheat flour soaked and fried), and both are served with *koko* (maize porridge and sugar).

The Yoruba, in southwestern Nigeria, also set maize or millet porridge alongside their breakfast bean dishes. Maize porridge, called *ògì*, is steamed in leaves and may be mixed with evaporated milk when eaten. There are again two alternative bean dishes. *Moin moin* is a steamed pudding made from black-eyed beans with onions and sweet and hot peppers. The black-eyed beans are soaked, ground to a paste, flavoured with dried crayfish and oil, and then steamed in leaves. Meat, fish and egg garnishes are added – seven of them would make *moin moin elemi meje*, or '*moin moin* with seven lives' – and the mixture is steamed in the sweet leaves of *ewe eran* or miracle berry (*Thaumatococcus daniellii*) or in banana leaves. The leaves are formed into a conical shape before they are steamed and the *moin moin* retains an inverted cone shape when served. The other bean dish scarcely differs from *kosai*: black-eyed beans are formed into a ball and deep fried in palm oil. Under its Yoruba name, *akara*, this dish is widely known across much of Cameroon, Nigeria, Benin, Togo and Ghana. Along with much else in West African cuisine, it crossed the Atlantic to Bahia state in Brazil with the slaves who were taken to work the sugar plantations. *Acarajé*, as it is known in Brazilian Portuguese, though no longer a breakfast staple, is now a speciality of the street food of the state capital, Salvador and is becoming known as far afield as Rio de Janeiro.

A rice and bean dish, as noted for Ghana above, is reincarnated all around the Caribbean under different names: again its origin in the region is traced to the transatlantic slave trade. In Nicaragua and Costa Rica it is *gallo pinto*, 'spotted hen', and in Cuba *moros y christianos*, 'Moors and Christians', both names taken from the variegated colour of the mixed red-purple beans and white rice (to which some, when the dish is cooked, add sour cream; others prefer a spicy brown sauce, Salsa Lizano). In Panama and El Salvador it is *casamiento*, in Puerto Rico *arroz con gandules*, in Colombia *calentado paisa* and in Peru *tacu tacu*. The same dish, though not typically breakfast, is *hoppin' John* in the southern United States. The Venezuelan *pabellón criollo* is a plate of rice, shredded beef and stewed black beans. The beef may give way to *chigüire* (capybara) or fish, which are permitted to Catholics during Lent. In its full form, with various additions and garnishes, *pabellón criollo* earns the title of national dish; cut down to its more basic breakfast form it is still substantial, especially if a fried egg is riding on it, making it *pabellón a caballo*.

The Savouries and Sweets

Two constituents of a breakfast are considered essential: the fluid, because we must drink, and the cereal, because we need carbohydrates and roughage. All else may be put down to nutritional planning – if nourishing breakfast foods allow more morning work and if as a result we take fewer such foods at supper; or wise frugality – if protein leftovers from the previous day's dinner are included in today's breakfast so as not to be wasted; or time-saving – if such additions make breakfast more palatable and therefore quicker to eat; or luxury.

Into these categories go, first of all, the milk that adds protein to many people's breakfast drink and cereal; salt, which may be added to porridge and may be present in breakfast cereals and savoury relishes; sugar, which is often added both to drinks and cereals. These are essential to the whole-day diet and they make breakfast more palatable: taken in moderation, they are part of the plan.

There are those in Britain who add no sugar to their porridge. There are those all over the world who breakfast simply on bread or rice or some other carbohydrate and tea. Even these unusual people ingest a little protein, a little salt, a very little sugar. For most people there is a great deal more to be included in the four categories sketched above, and the best that can be done here is to reduce their endless variety to some kind of order.

Take first sugar: a rich source of energy in the diet, a sensible ingredient in the breakfast of all who will face physical demands during the day that follows. Not all of us like sweet breakfasts, but many of us get the taste for them in childhood and never lose it. Some of us need them more than others. Sugar is added to a basic breakfast by mixing it, usually cane or beet sugar, into drinks; by adding it to cereals; or by including in one's menu sugar that has been converted into various forms. Maple syrup and honey are almost pure sugar; jellies, jams and marmalades are rich in it; fruit compotes, juices and nectars contain fruit sugars and are not uncommonly enriched with additional sugar. Breakfast cereals, particularly those whose marketing is aimed at children, are heavily laden with sugar.

During the twentieth century sugary breakfasts became the norm in Europe and across most of the Americas. For this it is tempting to blame French food fashion, since in France it is a commonly accepted principle that one should not mix salty and sweet flavours, and the only breakfast salt most French people eat is the vestigial salt in their breads or pastries. Yet French breakfasts are only mildly sugary: there are those in France who add no sugar to their coffee and no jam to their croissants; there are even those who like no sweetness in their hot chocolate. The French fashion, if such it was, has spread to certain less moderate countries where breakfasters may take three spoonfuls of sugar per cup of tea and where they may conceal their bread and butter behind an opaque screen of jam.

As for salt, the small quantity contained in most breads and porridges is outweighed by the amount in savoury relishes eaten at breakfast time. Even in Europe, salt mounts up, in cheese, in salted and dried

Marmite on toast. A favourite throughout the British Empire, Marmite was a very good way to use up the world's surplus of brewer's yeast.

meat and fish, in pickled vegetables. In the British dominions salt is lavishly ingested on every knife-blade of Marmite and its relatives (offspring of Justus Liebig's great nineteenth-century idea for re-using brewer's yeast). But most breakfasters consume these foods moderately. The commonest breakfast in the world is probably rice with a very little, very salty relish.

Breakfast is not the protein meal, but protein is taken in small quantities in cereal, in larger proportions in beans and peas and *nattō* and in larger proportions still in milk, cheese, eggs, fish and meat. Breakfast is not the fat meal, but oil is used wherever breakfast foods are fried; there is fat in pastries and there is plenty of fat in milk and salt pork.

The real nature of breakfast does not fully emerge from these generalizations. Its nature follows rather from its Neolithic origins. On the one hand it has to be prepared quickly, by and for people who have no time to waste on it. It must therefore be predictable, the choice of ingredients not the result of impulse or gastronomic cogitation but taken from what is available. For each household the stores remain relatively unchanging: they are there not for any single day but for a whole season or year. From this it follows that the breakfast habits of any household will be monotonous: while different dishes may be consumed every day for dinner, breakfast is likely to consist of the same dishes daily, or a very few that alternate on a predictable cycle.

And yet in any complex post-Neolithic community each household has different resources, different tastes and different needs in terms of what goes into store. Therefore, looking beyond the level of an individual family unit, the breakfast habits of any complex community will be extremely varied. Although the variety today is greatly increased by the spread of cultivated crops to new regions and by international trade, everything suggests that this always was the nature of breakfast: it is certainly true of regions of the world that have relatively little

Century egg or thousand-year egg congee.

exposure to international trade and relatively little buying power in world food markets.

The geography of breakfast beverages and cereals can just about be sketched. There are after all not so very many possibilities. But the geography of breakfast relishes, the savouries and sweets, the proteins and fats, cannot be encompassed in any reasonable space. To demonstrate this I might begin to name a couple of typical breakfast choices for each region of the modern world: it would be easy to complete a list of several hundred items, and I would still have touched the breakfasts of only a small minority in any country. Avoiding in this paragraph any foods mentioned elsewhere in the text, in China you might taste thousand-year eggs at breakfast; in Japan roasted aubergine; in Korea seasoned vegetables including ferns and wild greens (*chwinamul*), or clear vegetable soup flavoured with dried pollack; in Cambodia pig's blood congee; in northern India rice puddings, *firni* and *jarda*; in Pakistan halva and a chickpea and potato curry, or egg *khagina*, scrambled egg with vegetables and spices; in Afghanistan rice with spinach; in Iran *panir* cheese and walnuts; in Syria a morning salad of cucumbers, tomatoes, onions, mint and olive oil; in Jordan lamb sausage; in Libya tuna or a sweet *asida* cake dressed with date syrup; in Morocco *amlou*, a dip of toasted almonds, argan oil and honey; in Ghana sugar bread; in Nigeria coconut, peanuts and cashew nuts with your cassava porridge; in Spain *sobrasada*, a spreadable raw-cured spiced sausage; in Turkey clotted water buffalo cream; in Greece savoury pastries such as *tyropita* filled with cheese or *spanakopita* with spinach (see Recipes section); in the southern Balkans yogurt and honey, and in Croatia *sir i vrhnje* (cottage cheese with sour cream and spices; in Serbia open sandwiches with prosciutto, feta cheese and pickles; in Hungary hot dogs with mustard; in Poland *twarozek* (curd cheese with herbs); in Sweden caviar; in the Netherlands *chocoladevlokken* (chocolate flakes) and *stroop* (caramel spread) and *kokosbrood* (sliced coconut squares); in Italy *tramezzino* (a bread sandwich filled with tuna and tomato), and in Sicily *iris* (a deep-fried chocolate pastry); in France *pain aux raisins*; in Mexico *menudo* (tripe stew) and *barbacoa* (steamed beef or lamb); in Britain perhaps tinned baked beans and perhaps fried bread, and in Scotland smoked haddock boiled in milk

Greek *evzones* (elite light infantry) at breakfast in Larissa shortly before the outbreak of the Greco-Turkish War of 1897, from *The Graphic*, 24 April 1897.

and oatcakes with marmalade, in Northern Ireland fried soda bread and potato bread, potato scones, and black pudding; in Australia fresh fruit; in the u.s red eye gravy, shrimp mixed with hominy grits, scrapple, pork roll, fried chicken wings and catfish.

The Traveller's Breakfast

As we have seen, breakfasts may show extreme variety across a community and in neighbouring communities. This is why, before the advent of international hotels, the breakfasts of any long-distance traveller are likely to have been completely different every day.

Hence the breakfast that Edward Spencer Mott enjoyed in the late nineteenth century in Malta, and considered to be 'a bona-fide

Mediterranean breakfast', consisting as it did 'principally of red mullet and strawberries', might not be the breakfast that another traveller would have found there the following day.

Hence the breakfasts that Fanny Erskine, known after her marriage to a Spanish diplomat as Frances Calderón de la Barca, enjoyed during her visit to Mexico in the early 1840s seem from her descriptions to have been different almost every day as she and her husband travelled further off the beaten track. She justifies, incidentally, Conan Doyle's belief that 'Scotchwomen' have a good idea of breakfast: she writes about her breakfasts frequently and with well-judged praise. She clearly shows how Spanish breakfasts had been transformed in their New World environment and at the same time how travellers must adapt to their surroundings. At Jalapa (Xalapa-Enríquez), where we had better begin, 'our breakfast was delicious', she reports. 'Such fresh eggs, and fresh butter, and good coffee and well-fried chickens; moreover such good bread and peculiarly excellent water, that we fell very much in love with

'Picturesque San Antonio', Texas, c. 1890. A Mexican family is preparing breakfast using a primitive corn mill.

Jalapa.' So far, so ordinary: only the chicken would seem unusual at an English or Scottish breakfast, and even that might have been allowed as a variant where pork or beef were normal. Breakfast surprises commenced, not many days later, at La Ventilla, where Madame Calderón de la Barca and her husband were given 'a tolerable breakfast, hunger making chile and garlic supportable'. But she could not yet bring herself to drink *pulque*. If nectar was imbibed by the gods of Olympus, *pulque*, she decided, must be the beverage of Pluto in Hades. At the monastery of Tacuba they were served with 'a very nice breakfast, simple, but good; fish from the lake, different preparations of eggs, *riz-au-lait*, coffee and fruit'. A little further on, near Naucalpan, they visited the famous shrine of the Virgen de los Remedios, found an excellent breakfast prepared, 'and here, for the first time, I conceived the possibility of not disliking *pulque*'. But the most varied single breakfast in the whole memoir comes after these, when she was good and ready for it. This is the one to which she was invited after visiting a shrine at Santiago in central Mexico:

We found a tent prepared for us, formed of boughs of trees . . . and beautifully ornamented with red blossoms and scarlet berries. We sat down upon heaps of white moss, softer than any cushion. The Indians had cooked meat under the stones for us, which I found horrible, smelling and tasting of smoke. But we had also boiled fowls, and quantities of burning chile, hot tortillas, atole, or *atolli*, as the Indians call it, a species of cakes made of very fine maize and water, and sweetened with sugar or honey; *embarrado*, a favourite composition of meat and chile, very like mud, as the name imports, which I have not yet made up my mind to endure; quantities of fresh *tunas*, *granaditas*, bananas, *aguacates*, and other fruits, besides *pulque*, *à discretion*. The other people were assembled in circles under the trees, cooking fowls and boiling eggs in a gipsy fashion, in caldrons, at little fires made with dry branches; and the band, in its intervals of tortillas and *pulque*, favored us with occasional airs. After breakfast, we walked out amongst the Indians, who had formed a sort of temporary market, and were selling

pulque, chia, roasted chestnuts, yards of baked meat, and every
kind of fruit.

The *tunas,* incidentally, are not fish but prickly pears (specifically *Opuntia
ficus-indica*).

It is interesting to note that Fanny Calderón ate only what she chose.
At La Ventilla she refused *pulque.* At the shrine of the Virgen de los
Remedios she had learned to like it, or at least to accept it. At the shrine
at Santiago *pulque* had become normal but *embarrado* was as yet to be
rejected, and she shows incidentally that she is quite aware of the
process of acculturation and its effect on her own food choices. This
is brutal realism: this is exactly what is done by travellers and those
who have temporarily to take breakfast where they are not at home.
In Kingsley Amis's *Lucky Jim* the hero, living in lodgings, has to
make the best of the breakfast available to him, the eggs and bacon,
the 'explosive toast', the 'diuretic coffee'. He is free to choose and will
choose none of these. There is a remaining choice, as familiar as it is
tasteless. 'He circled the table like one trying to evade the smoke from
a bonfire, then sat down heavily and saturated a plate of cornflakes
with bluish milk.' But the traveller may have no choice at all: it is food
or no food, and that is how it may have been when Samuel Pepys and
companion, on the way back from Cambridge, as quoted in chapter
Two, 'had some red herrings to our breakfast' while Pepys's boots were
being mended.

Modern hotels know all about this. They will offer the usual national
choices; if they hope for an international clientele they will offer *Continental breakfast* (vaguely what a French bar might rustle up) and *English*
or *British* or *American breakfast* (vaguely as these are imagined) and
orange juice for luck, and whatever local product may be supposed to
tickle the international palate, such as fresh creamy yogurt and honey
in Greece. Those who cater for sea travellers and cruisers will offer as
much as they can in the full knowledge that little of it will be eaten: what
is eaten may well come back to haunt the eater, and all must be paid for.
'On the *Stella*' (in Evelyn Waugh's *Labels*) breakfast included 'besides
all the dishes usually associated with that meal, such solid fare as
goulash and steak and onions'. Edward Spencer Mott, 'experiencing

the restless, exasperating roll of the Bay of Biscay, and trying my utmost
to keep from falling out of the berth on to my head' was offered at
breakfast time the unwanted choice between liver and bacon and 'a
nice fat chop'. Fanny Calderón, on her way to Mexico, found that breakfast on shipboard offered 'every variety of fish, meat, fowl, fruit, sauces
and wines'.

In most parts of the world breakfast is expected even of the hotels
that don't boast of their lunches and dinners. Even so, the British Isles
are almost unique in that the expression 'bed and breakfast' gives a
name to what guest houses (and some hotels) claim to offer. *Lit et petit
déjeuner* doesn't have the same ring to it, and the nearest real French
equivalent, *chambres d'hôtes*, leaves both bed and breakfast unspecified.
In Dutch the expression *Logies en ontbijt* has been tried: it hasn't caught
on, and the English words are used instead. In Canada, New Zealand,
Australia and the u.s. the phrase 'bed and breakfast' is commonly seen,
but some would certainly claim that the British breakfast, as experienced
in a British bed and breakfast, has found no rival.

I end this survey of breakfast from a geographical perspective with
the case of Hugh Clapperton. His *Journal of a Second Expedition into the
Interior of Africa* was published fourteen years before Fanny Calderón's
memoir. Clapperton breakfasted one morning with the Sultan of Baussa,
a small state on the banks of the Quorra:

> This morning when I was with the sultan, his breakfast was
> brought in, which I was asked to partake of. It consisted of a
> large grilled water-rat with the skin on, some very fine boiled rice,
> with dried fish stewed in palm oil, and fried or stewed alligators'
> eggs, and fresh Quorra water. I eat some of the stewed fish and
> rice, and they were much amused at my not eating the rat and
> the eggs.

In 1854 the food writer John Doran quoted this West African breakfast, adding, without the slightest textual justification, 'The Prince, who
gave this public breakfast in honour of a foreign commoner, was disgusted at the fastidious super-delicacy of his guest', thus turning the
story into a diplomatic incident. It was in truth a fine example of the

A Continental breakfast. The glass of fruit-juice is a non-traditional addition. Many would dispense with the butter and jam, instead dipping the croissant in a big cup of chocolate or *café-au-lait*.

almost infinite variety of breakfast relishes (water-rat does not otherwise occur in this book) and of the adaptability of breakfasters: just like a modern tourist who manages to compose a palatable meal at the un-predictable buffet of a hotel breakfast-room, Clapperton left aside those items that he preferred not to face and chose for himself the constituents of his own adequate – if not perfect – breakfast.

Henri de Toulouse-Lautrec, *The Hangover* (*Gueule de Bois*), *c.* 1888, oil on canvas.

four

Variables

If you like your breakfast you mustn't ask the cook too
many questions, I answered.

Oliver Wendell Holmes,
The Poet at the Breakfast-table (1872)

Time

'The early bird catcheth the worm', we have been told (ever since
1605 at least, when the great historian William Camden wrote this
proverb down); in Romanian, when this is what they mean, they say
vulpea care doarme nu prinde găini, the sleeping wolf gets no hens.
Good advice begins even before breakfast.

> Early to bed and early to rise
> Makes a man healthy, wealthy and wise,

or so I remember being admonished during that adolescent period
when there always seemed to be better things to do than get out of bed.
The words are easily enough subverted. 'Early to rise and early to bed
makes a male healthy and wealthy and dead', wrote James Thurber in
'The Shrike and the Chipmunks'. 'Early to bed and early to rise makes
a man stupid and blind in the eyes' is the version favoured by Mazer
Rackham, the grey eminence of Orson Scott Card's science fiction tale
of 1985, *Ender's Game*. In its proper form the proverb was already
familiar in the days of Benjamin Franklin, who inserted it in his annual

Poor Richard's Almanac (1736) and recycled it in *The Way to Wealth*. The many who believe it goes back no further than Franklin are mistaken: Franklin learned it, if not at his mother's knee, then from John Ray's *English Proverbs* (1670) or from John Clarke's *Paroemiologia Anglo-Latina* (1639) or some intermediate source.

In the impenetrable shadows behind those works lies Anthony Fitzherbert's not-very-rhythmical translation, in the *Book of Husbandry* already quoted in chapter One, of the Latin tag that he had heard at grammar school. '*Sanat, sanctificat et ditat surgere mane*', he recites, and adds his English prose version, 'that is to say, "Early rising maketh a man whole in body, wholer in soul and richer in goods."' The Latin hexameter already gives exactly the same meaning as the later English verse couplet (except that the 'early to bed' idea is not yet present) and the Latin is certainly the older of the two: it comes from a set of versified medieval rules on health, *Regimen sanitatis Salernitanum*.

One obediently rises early, but how soon does one take one's breakfast? The answer is that in a northern winter, in which only eight hours separate sunset from sunrise, you must be prepared to eat before dawn breaks. These are Fitzherbert's own instructions, intended for farmers and smallholders. 'Be up betime,' he insists, 'and break thy fast before day, that thou mayest be all the short winter's day about thy business.' The eighteenth-century Spanish traveller Manuel Gonzalez observed that English children ate after dawn in summer and before dawn in winter: they have breakfast, he writes, 'at half an hour past six in the morning in the summer-time, and at half an hour past seven in the winter'. The seasonal difference is in itself interesting: it goes about halfway towards complying with the variation between summer sunrise and winter sunrise, clearly doing so because people could get up, eat and travel a familiar route before dawn but (until modern developments in artificial lighting) could generally not begin serious work at that time.

It is exactly these constraints and compromises with the seasons to which François Rabelais alludes in describing the morning routine of his temporary hero, the gross Gargantua: 'He ordinarily woke between eight and nine o'clock, whether it was daylight or not. That was the ruling of his old tutors, who quoted the words of David to him: *Vanum est vobis ante lucem surgere*.' Yes, the Psalms of David certainly say this

('In vain you rise up early and go late to rest . . .') but the psalmist goes on to explain his meaning: all effort is in vain if God's favour is lacking. It was naughty of Rabelais – who knew very well what he was doing – to take this biblical verse as if it were a general rule, and clever to add the clause 'whether it was daylight or not', exactly what one might say when praising the daily routine of someone who rises early. But in France it is always daylight before nine o'clock.

Having woken, Gargantua rolled around in bed awhile, then he 'shat, pissed, brought up phlegm, belched, farted, yawned, spat, coughed, hiccuped, sneezed, blew his nose like an archdeacon, and then breakfasted to overcome the dew and bad air: fine fried tripe, fine grills, fine hams, fine roast kid and plenty of morning soups'. These latter, these *soupes de prime*, were the correct early breakfasts for monks and nuns, who were allowed, after their six o'clock prayers, not bread dipped in wine (like other people) but bread dipped in *bouillon* or cooking liquor. Monks breakfasted on this alone, but Gargantua clearly enjoyed a much meatier breakfast.

The respectable timetable, then, was to get up and have breakfast at dawn or soon afterwards in summer, and not long before dawn in winter. This is the meaning of Martial's epigram, from classical Rome, in which a friend is urged,

> *Surgite: iam vendit pueris ientacula pistor*
> *Cristataeque sonant undique lucis aves.*

> Get up! The baker's already selling the slaves their breakfast,
> and larks are announcing daylight all around us.

Other scenes suggest that at a Mediterranean latitude, even if people need to get up before dawn, they are not likely to break their fast until the sun is already up. That is the implication of the fictional scene in the *Odyssey* with which this book opened. It cannot be proved that the scene is adopted from oral tradition but it is likely, and this would imply that it is intended to be a generalized sketch of a breakfast on the farm. Eumaios has sent the herdsmen out with the pigs to pasture; he and his guest are at work as the sun rises, preparing breakfast which the herdsmen will share when they return from their early morning task. A similar timetable is suggested by the story told in John's Gospel. The disciples have been at work through the night without any result; they see the stranger standing on the shore when dawn comes. Their breakfast follows soon after.

The question of the time at which breakfast is taken is of special interest to Muslims in the month of Ramadan. During that period religious observance requires fasting throughout the hours of daylight. It's advisable, therefore, to eat something substantial before dawn, because the next meal will not come until after sunset. The pre-dawn meal, which is a breakfast in all the ordinary English senses of the word, is called *suhur* (or in some countries *sahri*). But the meal that is taken immediately after sunset, as a preparation for the main meal that will follow late in the evening, can also properly be called a breakfast, because the long daytime fast is being broken. This early evening meal is *iftar*. Observant Muslims have been looking forward to it all day with pleasurable anticipation, and some will have found it appropriate to sit and enjoy the sight of the *iftar* for a few minutes before sunset comes; at the correct moment, however, it is important to begin to eat. Among favourite items in the *iftar* menu are dates. Muhammad himself ate these as breakfast and instructed others to do the same:

Abu Hurayrah narrated: 'The Prophet, peace be upon him, said: "Religion will continue to prevail as long as people hasten to break the fast, because the Jews and the Christians delay doing so."' . . . Salman ibn Amir narrated: 'The Prophet, peace be upon him, said: "When one of you is fasting, he should break his fast with dates; if he cannot get any dates, then with water, for water is purifying."' Anas ibn Malik narrated: 'The Apostle of Allah, peace be upon him, used to break his fast before praying with some fresh dates; if there were no fresh dates, he had a few dried dates, and if there were no dried dates, he took some mouthfuls of water.'

Fiction sometimes demonstrates a difference in timetable between the breakfasts of those who work and those who have a more leisurely day. In Maria Edgeworth's *The Absentee*, the narrative of a self-consciously upper-class breakfast in Grosvenor Square is cleverly orchestrated to demonstrate this very point:

> But just as she was rising from the breakfast-table, in came Sir Terence O'Fay, and, seating himself quite at his ease, in spite of Lady Clonbrony's repulsive looks, his awe of Lord Colambre having now worn off –
>
> 'I'm tired,' said he, 'and have a right to be tired; for it's no small walk I've taken for the good of this noble family this morning. And, Miss Nugent, before I say more, I'll take a cup of *ta* from you, if you please.'

Regaled with tea (Edgeworth is good on accents, incidentally: *ta* was outmoded in London but normal among Irishmen) Sir Terence narrates his breathless race across London, first of all to visit 'the little solicitor that lives in Crutched Friars . . . he was very genteel, though he was taken on a sudden, and from his breakfast, which an Englishman don't like particularly'; then, taking the first coach he found, to Long Acre for a triumphant negotiation in a moneylender's office; then to Grosvenor Square where the tea was still hot. Which, as Arnold Palmer observed in *Movable Feasts*, shows that the little solicitor in Crutched Friars breakfasted as much as an hour and a half before the Clonbronys did. The same differential in twentieth-century Australia is brought out in Henry Handel Richardson's *The Way Home*, in which

> Mrs Devine herself, clad in a voluminous paisley gown, her nightcap bound under her chin, was early astir: she gave her husband, who rose at dawn to work among his flowers – as he had once worked among his market produce – breakfast at eight, before he left for town. But if you belonged to the elite, were truly *bon ton*, you did not descend till the morning was half over.

Her house guests, whatever their frustration, are not permitted to breakfast till after ten o'clock.

'Late for Breakfast', *c.* 1901, by the photographer William Herman Rau (1855–1920).

Whenever one breakfasts, let it at least be at the same time every day. The discomfort of a sudden alteration is nicely evoked in Kingsley Amis's *Lucky Jim*:

> He didn't like having to breakfast so early. There was something about Miss Cutler's cornflakes, her pallid fried eggs or bright red bacon . . . which, much better than bearable at nine o'clock, his usual breakfast-time, seemed at eight-fifteen to summon from all the recesses of his frame every lingering vestige of crapulent headache, every relic of past nauseas.

Somewhere in the early to mid morning will come the breakfasts that are consumed at a resting point after a journey has begun, and they will perhaps be more filling if there is by that time more space to fill. Such was the Hebridean breakfast, 'pretty early in the morning', in James Boswell's 'Account of the Escape of the Young Pretender', a narrative of Prince Charles Edward Stuart's flight in 1746 towards lifelong exile in France after the failure of the Jacobite rebellion. The prince's guide was Malcolm McLeod, with the prince pretending to be his servant, 'Lewis Caw'. After travelling through most of the night they reached the temporary refuge of McLeod's sister's house on the small island of Raasay, which lies between Skye and the mainland coast.

She set down to her brother a plentiful Highland breakfast. Prince Charles acted the servant very well, sitting at a respectful distance, with his bonnet off. Malcolm then said to him, 'Mr

Sir Edwin Henry Landseer RA, *A Highland Breakfast*, c. 1834, oil on canvas.

Caw, you have as much need of this as I have; there is enough
for us both; you had better draw nearer and share with me.'
Upon which he rose, made a profound bow, sat down at table
with his supposed master, and ate very heartily.

One wonders if this so-called Highland breakfast of 1746 was just
like the Scottish breakfast that earned Samuel Johnson's praise and
Boswell's complacency a generation later – or did it contain something
meatier than bread and marmalade?

It will be later in the morning that Apuleius' travellers pause for
some bread and cheese from a backpack after a walk of several miles:
'my knees are shaking and my feet are stumbling', says the narrator's
companion, who, so far from being revived by his breakfast, dies before
he has finished it. It is later, too, that Philip of France, in Boccaccio's
story, sits down to his breakfast after his morning ride to the Countess
of Montferrat's castle. It is very late in the morning when the paladin
Olivier, after a longer ride, consumes his unusual breakfast of cold
roast swan before the walls of Saragossa.

There are those who breakfast late even when not on a journey.
The fictional Gargantua is matched, indeed surpassed, by his country-
man, the diplomat Talleyrand, who (as quoted earlier) rose about
eleven o'clock and 'about half an hour afterwards made a light breakfast'.
Almost as late as that was the London breakfast to which Thomas
Babington Macaulay, a young politician soon to be an eminent historian,
was invited by the ageing statesman Lord Holland. Macaulay describes
it with pardonable pride in a letter to his sister, temporarily breaking
into dramatic verse:

> *Scene, the great entrance of Holland House. Enter Macaulay*
> *and two Footmen in livery.*
> FIRST FOOTMAN. Sir, may I venture to demand your name?
> Macaulay. Macaulay, and thereto I add M.P.
> And that addition, even in these proud halls,
> May well ensure the bearer some respect.
> SECOND FOOTMAN. And art thou come to breakfast with our
> Lord?

MACAULAY. I am, for so his hospitable will
And hers – the peerless dame ye serve – hath bade.
FIRST FOOTMAN. Ascend the stair, and thou above shalt find,
On snow-white linen spread, the luscious meal.
Exit Macaulay up stairs. – In plain English prose, I went this
morning to breakfast at Holland House. The day was fine,
and I arrived at twenty minutes after ten. After I had lounged
a short time in the dining-room, I heard a gruff good-natured
voice asking, 'Where is Mr Macaulay? Where have you put
him?' and in his arm-chair Lord Holland was wheeled in.

The breakfast itself (the menu quoted in chapter Two) can hardly have
got under way before eleven o'clock, given that Macaulay was shown
the apartments and the paintings before returning to the dining room.

Evelina, heroine of Fanny Burney's epistolary novel published 50
years earlier, also breakfasts late, but she has at least the excuse of
having taken a walk beforehand:

'Good God! Miss Anville, have you been out alone? Breakfast
has been ready some time, and I have been round the garden
in search of you.'

'Your Lordship has been very good,' said I; 'but I hope you
have not waited.'

'Not waited!' repeated he, smiling: 'Do you think we could
sit down quietly to breakfast, with the idea that you had run
away from us?'

She turns to dismiss her unofficial visitor, promising: 'Perhaps you
may be this way again to-morrow morning, – and I believe I shall
walk out before breakfast.' Late as breakfast must have been – and it
was the fault of Evelina and her visitor after all – it was not as late as
the London breakfast reported in an earlier letter in the same novel:
'Madame Duval rose very late this morning, and, at one o'clock, we
had but just breakfasted.'

Jane Austen in *Mansfield Park* meticulously chronicles Fanny's
tearful farewell to her brother William. The episode begins with the

question of when he will breakfast before leaving, and whether Fanny
will have breakfast with him:

> 'Well, then, Fanny, you shall not get up to-morrow before I go.
> Sleep as long as you can, and never mind me.'
> 'Oh! William.'
> 'What! Did she think of being up before you set off?'
> 'Oh! yes, sir,' cried Fanny, rising eagerly from her seat to be
> nearer her uncle; 'I must get up and breakfast with him. It will
> be the last time, you know; the last morning.'
> 'You had better not. He is to have breakfasted and be gone
> by half-past nine. Mr Crawford, I think you call for him at
> half-past nine?'
> Fanny was too urgent, however, and had too many tears
> in her eyes for denial; and it ended in a gracious 'Well, well!'
> which was permission.
> 'Yes, half-past nine,' said Crawford to William as the latter
> was leaving them, 'and I shall be punctual, for there will be
> no kind sister to get up for me . . .'

Number

Now it is curious that after the following morning's sad breakfast (which
will be quoted in chapter Five) Jane Austen timetables a 'second breakfast' half an hour later. She surely did not intend to imply that Fanny
would greedily and callously tuck in a second time (though a second cup
of tea might perhaps be allowed her while the slugabed members of
the household are taking their single, late breakfast). Jane Austen is, I
think, the first English author to have used the phrase 'second breakfast'.
She started something.

In a tradition that has grown and solidified from J.R.R. Tolkien's
time onwards it is now a commonplace among Ring enthusiasts that
Hobbits enjoy two breakfasts (whether or not that is true of Men). Bilbo
Baggins, in *The Hobbit*, soon after calming his nerves with a 'nice little
breakfast', 'was just sitting down to a nice little second breakfast in
the dining-room' when he was visited by Gandalf – hence we never

Gustav Wentzel, *Breakfast (Frokost),* 1882, oil on canvas.

find out what the second breakfast comprised. In the author's prologue
to *The Fellowship of the Ring,* immediate sequel to *The Hobbit,* we learn
that Hobbits 'eat, and drink, often and heartily, being fond of simple
jests at all times, and of six meals a day (when they could get them)'. The
hint is taken up in Peter Jackson's film version of *The Fellowship of the
Ring.* An almost throwaway original line – 'We will leave at once,' (said
by Aragorn after the Nazgûl's night attack on the inn at Bree), 'never
mind about breakfast: a drink and a bite standing will have to do' – is
expanded sententiously in the film script:

ARAGORN: Gentlemen, we do not stop till nightfall.
PIPPIN: What about breakfast?
ARAGORN: You've already had it.
PIPPIN: We've had one, yes. What about second breakfast?
MERRY: I don't think he knows about second breakfast, Pip.
PIPPIN: What about elevenses? Luncheon? Afternoon tea?

Dinner? Supper? He knows about them, doesn't he?

MERRY: I wouldn't count on it.

Hobbits are not an exact copy of humans, but in their liking for a second breakfast they strongly resemble certain humans known to Tolkien, Germanic philologist that he was. In Thomas Mann's novel *The Magic Mountain*, set among Germans in the decade preceding the First World War, second breakfasts are noticeably prominent. The usual term in modern Germany is *Zwischenmahlzeit*, the 'between-meal', though there are other regional names; in Austria it is usually *Jause*. The typical second breakfast in Munich, for those who indulge, is a local speciality, a white sausage, *Weisswurst*, prepared early in the morning to be eaten later with pretzels, mustard and wheat beer.

Britons, too, have been known to take *elevenses*. In the film version of *The Fellowship of the Ring*, just quoted, Pippin distinguished elevenses from second breakfast and it is notable that in this way Tolkien's six meals a day become Jackson's seven. This has been noted in Lord of the Rings fandom, and seven seems now to have been adopted as the official count. English elevenses, which for schoolchildren once consisted

Bavarian white sausages (*Weisswurst*) with sweet mustard and a pretzel. Prepared early the same morning (because the sausages do not keep), this is a typical second breakfast in Bavaria.

of the half-pint of milk of which Mrs Thatcher famously deprived them, is comparable to *Jause* and *Zwischenmahlzeit* and to the *panino* that Italian children often take as a mid-morning snack.

These are all examples of a second breakfast that is lighter than the first. When breakfasts come doubly it is equally common for the first to be the lighter one. The travellers whose late breakfasts are mentioned above might, for all we can know, have taken a 'morning draught' or 'rinsed their mouths' before setting out on their journeys. That is what Athenaios would suggest for ancient Greece in his careful distinctions quoted in chapter One between the Greek *akratisma*, early and light, and the *ariston*, later, bulkier and tending towards lunch – with the fragment of comedy dialogue that reinforced his point: "'The cook's preparing *ariston*.' 'Then how about having an *akratisma* with me?'" Alternatively (we don't know the context) this may have been a joke about immoderate greed: perhaps normal healthy ancient Greeks never took both meals on the same day.

This early, light breakfast, in any case, is the *chotī hāzirī* or 'little breakfast' or 'early tea' of British India; it is the *matar-o-bicho*, 'kill-the-worm', sometimes swallowed by Portuguese labourers before work begins; it is the nip of whisky that Samuel Johnson noted Scotsmen taking in the early morning, and the 'morning draught' taken by the Spanish fishermen observed by George Borrow, who might then take a heavy breakfast, *almuerzo*, at mid-morning. In Mexico, too, peasants used to have a bit of bread and a hot drink at dawn, followed by a mid-morning *desayuno* as generous as those described by Fanny Calderón. Among farmers in the United States a small 'first breakfast', such as toast and coffee, is still sometimes followed by a heartier second breakfast after the first round of chores are done. And are there not people in modern Britain who enjoy a cup of tea in bed before the daily grind?

Completing the story of second breakfast is brunch, a negation of the second breakfast idea, for it is a late morning meal preceded by nothing. Brunch can be dated precisely to the English naughty nineties (the 1890s, that is), when, after a heavy Saturday evening, there were some who found themselves unable to rise early on a Sunday morning. The solution was to take a nourishing meal, combining aspects of breakfast and lunch, some time before noon on Sunday morning. The idea was explained, and the word *brunch* apparently used for the first time, by Guy Beringer in the short-lived *Hunter's Weekly* in 1895:

> Why not a new meal, served around noon, that starts with tea or coffee, marmalade and other breakfast fixtures before moving along to the heavier fare? By eliminating the need to get up early on Sunday, brunch would make life brighter for Saturday-night carousers.

Beringer was properly credited for his great invention in *Punch* in August 1896: 'To be fashionable nowadays we must "brunch". Truly an excellent portmanteau word.' The anonymous *Punch* article has a distinction of its own: it is the first text in which Humpty Dumpty's special use of the word *portmanteau* is applied to a word not invented by Lewis Carroll. Within a decade the idea and name of brunch had crossed the Atlantic, receiving such a warm welcome that many soon thought of it as an American invention.

Love

Surgere mane, 'get up early', is a noble precept but, as we have seen, it isn't for everybody. The medieval poet Serlo of Wilton, a monk with a dry sense of humour, pasted the rule into his mnemonic poem on Latin words that have the same spelling and, while doing so, hinted at one of the best reasons for disobeying it: *'Care' dico 'mane', cum debeo surgere mane*: 'I say "stay, my love," when I ought to be getting up early.' Serlo probably remembered the classical poet Ovid's comment on the same subject in *Amores* (Ovid's love poems were appreciated by monks at least as much as any other readers):

> *Omnia perpeterer – sed surgere mane puellas*
> *Quis, nisi cui non est ulla puella, ferat?*

> I can forgive all the rest – but make girls get up early?
> Who but a man who doesn't have a girl of his own would do that?

These references serve as a reminder of one of the better recipes for an enjoyable breakfast: sharing it with a lover. Byron in the second canto of *Don Juan* surely had this thought in mind, as well as a wise proverb long ago cited by Terence (*Sine Cerere et Libero friget Venus*, 'Venus will freeze without Ceres and Bacchus' or, more practically, 'Love will go cold without food and drink'). 'Good lessons are also learnt from Ceres and from Bacchus, without whom Venus will not long attack us,' Byron observes as an aside, before taking up his story:

> When Juan woke, he found some good things ready,
> A bath, a breakfast, and the finest eyes
> That ever made a youthful heart less steady . . .
> Well – Juan, after bathing in the sea,
> Came always back to coffee and Haidee.

The shipwrecked Juan and his saviour Haidee are perhaps at this moment not yet lovers: clearly they soon will be, and in such a context an early breakfast is quite acceptable. Juan's arrives 'by daybreak – rather early for Juan, who was somewhat fond of rest'. The breakfast shared in D. H. Lawrence's *Lady Chatterley's Lover* by Connie and her lover, the gamekeeper Mellors, is at 'half past six: she had to be at the lane-end at eight. Always, always, always this compulsion on one! "I might make the breakfast and bring it up here; should I?" said Mellors; after which:

> She heard him making the fire, pumping water, going out at the back door. By and by came the smell of bacon, and at length he came upstairs with a huge black tray that would only just go through the door. He set the tray on the bed, and poured out the tea. Connie squatted in her torn nightdress, and fell on her food hungrily.

The intimate breakfasts of all other heroes pale before those of King Solomon. He had, after all, 700 wives, and although his early-morning meals are not mentioned in the Book of Kings, they are discussed, as is every other biblical detail about which the enquiring mind

Carl Larsson, *Frukost under stora björken*, 1896, watercolour. 'Breakfast under the big birch tree' appeared as an illustration in Larsson's memoir of family life, *Ett hem*, published in 1899.

might devise a question, in the medieval Hebrew commentaries. It was noted that 'Solomon's provision for one day was thirty measures of fine flour, and threescore measures of meal . . . and a hundred sheep.' If this were not to seem excessive it clearly needed some explanation, and Rabbi Judah's explanation perfectly suited the case. Every one of his wives 'prepared a breakfast – every wife every day – for each hoped Solomon would dine with her'.

If not taken with a lover, breakfast may recall an absent lover. So it does for Prince von Pückler-Muskau, who writes to his wife, describing a breakfast in Ireland, and continues, 'When shall we see each other again? when shall we breakfast under the three lime-trees, with the swans who so trustingly fed out of our hands, while your tame doves picked up the crumbs at our feet?' An earlier breakfast of his, at the inn at Llangollen, had been described more sensuously, ending with the telltale words: '*Je dévore déjà un oeuf. – Adieu.*' Yet even here, and in spite of the egg, homesickness left him hungry: he was at any rate ready after a short journey to accept an invitation to a 'second breakfast' the same morning with the lesbian ladies of Llangollen, Eleanor Butler and Sarah Ponsonby.

The more formal kind of breakfast, the kind that takes place in a breakfast room, may provide opportunity for flirtation if not for lovemaking. In Maria Edgeworth's *The Absentee*, Grace Nugent takes the chance to give much-needed support to young Colambre, who is the butt of sarcasm from both his parents for disappearing the previous evening:

> 'Good morning to you, my Lord Colambre,' said his mother, in a reproachful tone, the moment he entered; 'I am much obliged to you for your company last night' . . .
>
> 'I thank you, ma'am, for missing me,' said he, addressing himself to his mother; 'I stayed away but half an hour; I accompanied my father to St James's Street . . .'
>
> 'And, lest you should be jealous of that half-hour when he was accompanying me,' said Lord Clonbrony, 'I must remark, that, though I had his body with me, I had none of his mind; that he left at home with you ladies . . . for the deuce of two words did he bestow upon me . . .'
>
> 'Lord Colambre seems to have a fair chance of a pleasant breakfast,' said Miss Nugent, smiling; 'reproaches on all sides.'
>
> 'I have heard none on your side, Grace,' said Lord Clonbrony; 'and that's the reason, I suppose, he wisely takes his seat beside you.'

Comparable is the breakfast scene in Kingsley Amis's *Lucky Jim*, though the hero finds the breakfast room empty except for 'the Callaghan girl, sitting behind a well-filled plate . . . The remains of a large pool of sauce were to be seen . . . beside a diminishing mound of fried egg, bacon, and tomatoes. Even as he watched she replenished her stock of sauce with a fat scarlet gout from the bottle.' A hangover prevents him from matching her appetite.

A modern full English fried breakfast; traditionally this would not have included baked beans. But there's more if you're hungry. A preceding bowl of cereal or porridge; slices of toast with butter and marmalade to follow; tea with milk and sugar.

'Oh, I shall have to miss that. There's not time.'

'I shouldn't if I were you. They don't give you much for lunch here, you know.' . . .

'Wait a minute.' He darted back to the sideboard, picked up a slippery fried egg and slid it into his mouth whole . . . Chewing violently, he doubled up a piece of bacon and crammed it between his teeth, then signalled he was ready to move. Intimations of nausea circled round his digestive system.

The 'fat scarlet gout' identifies the sauce as tomato ketchup, indispensable garnish at every modern table at which the Great breakfast is attempted. But the most successful breakfast-table flirtation is that conducted (in the best possible taste) by the autocrat in Oliver Wendell Holmes's first breakfast dialogue. The autocrat, after all, is the man who knows what he wants and intends to have it:

The schoolmistress came down with a rose in her hair – a fresh June rose. She has been walking early; she has brought back two

"A young fellow
answering to the name of John"

others, one on each cheek. I told her so, in some such pretty
phrase as I could muster for the occasion. Those two blush-
roses I just spoke of turned into a couple of damasks.

'Will you walk out and look at those elms with me after
breakfast?' I said to the schoolmistress.

I am not going to tell lies about it, and say that she blushed,
as I suppose she ought to have done, at such a tremendous piece
of gallantry as that was for our boarding-house. On the contrary,
she turned a little pale, but smiled brightly and said, Yes, with
pleasure, but she must walk towards her school . . .

'This is the shortest way,' she said, as we came to a corner.
'Then we won't take it,' said I. The schoolmistress laughed a
little, and said she was ten minutes early, so she could go round.

Health

The most ancient known justification for taking breakfast is in the
form of that appeal to health (or, one might rather say, personal hygiene) that was expressed in the ancient Egyptian term for breakfast,

'mouth-cleansing'. A classical Roman breakfast, Latin *ientaculum*, was expected by some, at least, to serve the same healthy purpose. This is clear from an epigram by Martial:

> *Ne gravis hesterno fragres, Fescennia, vino,*
> *Pastillos Cosmi luxuriosa voras.*
> *Ista linunt dentes iantacula, sed nihil obstant,*
> *Extremo ructus cum redit a barathro.*

> So as not to be laden with the aroma of yesterday's wine,
>   Fescennia,
> you swallow Cosmus' expensive pastilles.
> Yes, that sort of breakfast cleans the teeth,
> but it does no good when a belch bubbles up from the
>   deepest gulch.

It is usually assumed that Martial changed the names in his less-flattering epigrams, of which this is certainly one, but he didn't pull his punches. Plenty of other early texts make it clear that cleansing the mouth and breath is one of the purposes of breakfast, and if there are two breakfasts, this is the special purpose of the earlier and lighter one. Among these is the *Regimen sanitatis Salernitanum* mentioned above. This versified set of medieval rules on health and diet was (falsely) rumoured to have been compiled by the assembled medical school of Salerno under the direction of the learned Arnold of Villanova and addressed to a certain king of England (according to the French manuscripts) or of France (according to the English manuscripts). The instructions on food and drink contained in this rulebook include a recommendation for a light breakfast – bread soaked in wine – and they also supply a medieval Latin name for this health-giving mixture:

> *Vippa* has twice two effects: it cleans the teeth, gives sharp sight, fills what is empty, empties what is full . . . It clears the digestion, it even cures bad breath, it sharpens the intellect.

Not long after the *Regimen* was compiled Boccaccio was telling the story of Geri Spini and the baker Cisti. Bread and wine formed the baker's breakfast, and while enjoying it he coughed ostentatiously to clear his throat. In the Don Quixote story, after Sancho has extracted supplies from his saddle-bags to provide breakfast for his master and himself, he 'rinsed his mouth'.

Mouth-rinsing aside, health may also be a reason for not taking breakfast at all. I have already quoted the Hippocratic text from classical Greece, *Ancient Medicine*, which said that 'eating once a day suits some healthy people, and they have made this their rule', adding that 'it does not matter to most people which rule they adopt, eating once a day or taking lunch'. In that account of healthy ancient lifestyles breakfast was conspicuous by its absence. Ancient dietary writings had a long vogue, and it is surely out of familiarity with such handbooks that Humphrey Brooke, in seventeenth-century England, advises his readers not to eat breakfast: 'The previous night's meal and the energy expended in . . . assimilating it is what causes heaviness and weariness in the limbs. The remedy for a sluggish morning is abstinence, not food.'

A Pennsylvanian nutritionist of the late nineteenth century, Edward Hooker Dewey, gave similar advice even more forcefully in *The No Breakfast Plan and the Fasting-cure*. This discursive text gives the reader the strong impression that Dewey was reacting against the very breakfast habits Paul Pierce was about to recommend (in *Breakfasts and Teas*, quoted in chapter Two). The harrowing chapter 'Personal experience of the author as a dyspeptic – His first experience without a breakfast' opens with a confession: 'The breakfasts in my house were of a character that, without ham, sausage, eggs, steaks, or chops, they would not have been considered worth spending time over.' Weighed down one day by an unusually arduous breakfast, Dewey met an old friend who told him about European food, notably 'the exceedingly light breakfasts customary in all the great centres where he had been. They consisted only of a roll and a cup of coffee.' Dewey tried it, and 'a forenoon resulted of such comfort of body, such cheer, and such mental and physical energy as had never been realized since my young manhood was happy in the blessed unconsciousness of having a stomach that, no matter how large or how numerous the daily meals, never complained.' He means,

I think, that his roll and coffee made him feel young and frisky. He began to prescribe this (or, rather, even less) to his hospital patients, and none of them died of it. 'The no-breakfast plan was not so very long in becoming known over the entire city.' The city in question was Meadville in Pennsylvania.

Dewey's fellow medics disapproved, but his prescriptions worked: 'A man in the early prime of life had reached a condition in which he habitually rejected every breakfast', and while other doctors were puzzled, Dewey immediately saw that 'if no breakfasts were put into his stomach none would have to be thrown up'. The patient took his advice, afterwards observing 'that he began to get well as soon as I began to talk to him'. The rule that Dewey had at last in this way evolved can hardly be faulted:

> It is the **sense of relish**, of flavor, that is behind all the woes of indigestion, and not the sense of hunger. The sweetened foods; the pies, cakes, puddings, etc., that are eaten merely from a sense of relish after the sense of hunger has become fully sated, and generally by far more of the plainer foods than waste demands, is the wrecking sin at all but the humblest tables. **Rapid eating**, by which there is imperfect solution of the tougher solids and a filling of the stomach before the hunger sense can naturally be appeased, is the additional evil to insure serious consequences to the stomach and brain.

I have quoted the dyspeptic Dewey at such length because a great number of twenty-first-century people adopt what Dewey called a 'No Breakfast Diet' for reasons that are no more coherent than these.

Breakfasts – at least any breakfasts that include something more than bread and water – may be reduced nearer to the minimum by the demands of religion. Twice James Boswell, in his *Life of Johnson*, refers to Johnson's 'discipline' at Easter. In 1778, he observes mischievously 'that although it was a part of his discipline, on this most abstemious fast, to take no milk in his tea, yet when Mrs Desmoulins inadvertently poured it in, he did not reject it'. On Good Friday in 1783 'I found him at breakfast, in his usual manner upon that day, drinking tea without milk, and eating a cross bun to prevent faintness', a reminder that this is the reason hot cross buns were invented. During her travels in nineteenth-century Mexico, Frances Calderón de la Barca noted that when she and her husband were provided with breakfast at the monastery of Tacuba – fish from the lake, eggs, rice cooked in milk, coffee and fruit – the monks themselves did not partake of the meal.

Whether adults take heavy breakfasts, or no breakfasts at all, and whether or not they consider the implications for their own health, they have long held strong views about what kind of breakfasts children should eat. This was clearly the case already in 1730, when Manuel Gonzalez visited England and noted: 'The children are dieted in the following manner: They have every morning for their breakfast bread and beer.' Beer in due course disappeared from children's breakfast tables; in *Tom Brown's Schooldays*, Tom, on his way to school and faced with the waiter's question 'Tea or coffee, sir?', is familiar with both and knows at once which he will choose ('coffee is a treat to him, tea is not').

In Gwen Raverat's *Period Piece* she recalls her early twentieth-century childhood in Cambridge (she was Charles Darwin's granddaughter). Chapter Three of her memoir is entitled 'Theories' to signal the weighty importance of these in her upbringing. Theories – her mother's in particular – determined her breakfasts:

> Surely our feeding was unnecessarily austere? We had porridge for breakfast, with salt, not sugar; and milk to drink. Porridge always reminds me of having breakfast alone with my father, when I was so small that I put the porridge into the spoon with my fingers, while he told me stories in French . . . There was toast and butter, but I never had anything stronger for breakfast, till I tasted bacon for the first time in my life when I went to stay with Frances, at the age of nearly ten.

Sweets of almost every kind were outlawed for the children of this academic Cambridge family: 'Sugar was thought to be unwholesome; and fruit, though a pleasant treat, rather dangerous'; 'Jam might have weakened our moral fibre'. She always writes the word with a capital J to emphasize its symbolic significance:

Albert Anker, *Kinderfrühstück* ('Children's breakfast'), 1879: Anker, a Swiss artist, was celebrated for his genre scenes in watercolour.

Twice a week we had, at the end of breakfast, one piece of toast, spread with a thin layer of that dangerous luxury, Jam. But, of course, not butter, too. Butter and Jam on the same bit of bread would have been an unheard-of indulgence – a disgraceful orgy. The queer thing is that we none of us like it to this very day.

Guidance

Many people, in common with Gwen Raverat's parents, have appealed to beliefs about health as a reason for the choice of particular foods at breakfast. We recall 'the renowned fortifying chocolate, light yet nutritious, prepared with Persian *salep*' that Grimod de la Reynière undertook to puff on behalf of a chemist turned chocolatier in the Faubourg Saint-Germain. 'The ladies who read this *Almanach*', he continued shamelessly, 'will thank us for having revealed to them a doubly precious secret: how to regain their health, retain their beauty, and at the same time enjoy a breakfast of excellent chocolate.' This salep was the powdered root of an orchid that has at times had a reputation as an aphrodisiac. It is still enjoyed, a stimulating alternative to coffee, as an early-morning winter drink in Turkey. Salep is now forgotten in France and England, yet Rodway's coffee-house at Billingsgate (Henry Mayhew's description in 1851 was quoted in chapter One) was 'a clean, orderly, and excellent establishment, kept by a man, I was told, who had risen from a saloop stall'. Rodway, in other words, used to sell this same strengthening drink on the streets of London.

Grimod de la Reynière was quoted in chapter Two on his history of how the early French breakfast was transformed in his time into the modern French lunch. I avoided quoting the fantastically lavish menus that he ascribes to this 'inconsequential' meal. But even in those breakfast menus Grimod started a trend. During the nineteenth century those in France and England who took seriously the food books they read were encouraged to provide lavish breakfasts for their households. *The Book of Household Management* (first edition, 1861) is by far the best known of them and, to be fair to Isabella Beeton, her advice on 'the comfortable meal called breakfast' is – in the very first edition – brief and almost modest, if we are prepared to forgive the affectation (borrowed from Grimod) of listing a whole banquet after claiming that one will do no such thing:

2144. It will not be necessary to give here a long bill of fare of cold joints, &c., which may be placed on the side-board, and do duty at the breakfast-table. Suffice it to say, that any cold meat the larder may furnish, should be nicely garnished, and be placed on the buffet. Collared and potted meats or fish, cold game or poultry, veal-and-ham pies, game-and-rump-steak pies, are all suitable dishes for the breakfast-table; as also cold ham, tongue, &c. &c.

2145. The following list of hot dishes may perhaps assist our readers in knowing what to provide for the comfortable meal called breakfast. Broiled fish, such as mackerel, whiting, herrings, dried haddocks, &c.; mutton chops and rump-steaks, broiled sheep's kidneys, kidneys à la maître d'hôtel, sausages, plain rashers of bacon, bacon and poached eggs, ham and poached eggs, omelets, plain boiled eggs, oeufs-au-plat, poached eggs on toast, muffins, toast, marmalade, butter, &c. &c.

2146. In the summer, and when they are obtainable, always have a vase of freshly-gathered flowers on the breakfast-table, and, when convenient, a nicely-arranged dish of fruit: when strawberries are in season, these are particularly refreshing; as also grapes, or even currants.

The book had a life of its own, continuing to appear in new editions for a hundred years, and the advice of *Mrs Beeton* became more elaborate with every decade, adding grand breakfast menus for large parties, small parties, families and (at the extreme outer limit of the editors' vision) economical families. And there were other household books. Appearing on the market almost at the same moment as Mrs Beeton's first edition were the first books devoted entirely to breakfast. The authors unanimously boasted that they were aiming at economy. In truth they urged on their readers ever larger, more varied, elaborate and costly morning meals. These books were certainly bought – M. L. Allen's *Breakfast Dishes for Every Morning of Three Months*, an early classic in the genre, ran to 24 editions between 1884 and 1915 – but how seriously their readers took them is hard to know. *The Breakfast Book* (1865), a very early example of the genre, enumerates four kinds of breakfast: 'The family breakfast', '*Déjeuner à la fourchette*', 'Cold collation' and at the top of the range:

> The *ambigu* . . . having resemblance to a dinner, only that
> everything is placed upon the table at once . . . Our every-day
> breakfasts are in a small way served *en ambigu*, inasmuch as
> broiled fish, cold pasties, devilled bones, boiled eggs, cold ham,
> etc., all appear together.

'Our every-day breakfasts', 'in a small way': these are almost exactly the same modest notes that Grimod de la Reynière reached for as he neared the climax of his evocation of the *déjeuners* of revolutionary Paris. The late Victorian and Edwardian editions of the *Book of Household Management*, like the specialized breakfast books, included illustrations of table layouts, as if to complete the conversion of breakfast – a meal that has its own purpose, routine and perfection, and deserves to retain them – into a frozen, reheated, silver-service semblance of dinner.

From our perspective these elaborations can be seen to have continued on their autonomous way at the very same period that an utterly contrasting approach to breakfast was being urged. In the very long run, as we now know, it was this contrasting approach that prevailed.

The insistence on cereal foods as a healthy breakfast choice has a long history. In the eighteenth century George Cheyne in his *Essay on Health and Long Life* advised people whose life was contemplative rather than active to eat nothing till eleven o'clock, 'then to take some agreeable breakfast of vegetable food' – which I take to be a recommendation of bread, not cabbage. If that is what it is, it is more liberal than John Doran in *Table Traits*, published a century later. 'Solid breakfasts,' Doran advised his Victorian readers, are 'fit only for those who have much solid exercise to take after it; otherwise heartburn may be looked for.' Doran went further: it was a popular error, he insisted, 'that a breakfast cannot be, unless bread and butter be of it. Avoid new bread and spongy rolls; look on muffins and crumpets . . . and hot buttered toast as of equally wicked origin. Dry toast is the safest morning food.'

It was soon after Doran's first edition (1854), and before his second (1865), that a new genre of breakfast foods burst into existence. In 1863 James Caleb Jackson, proprietor of a sanatorium with the comforting name of Our Home on the Hillside in Dansville, New York, invented Granula and employed it as part of his patients' tightly restricted diet. Rich in bran, it became edible only after overnight soaking. If Granula sounds unfamiliar this is because its name and nature have since changed, but its direct descendants, Grape-Nuts, are still crunched today.

Other innovations also sprang from Jackson's invention. At the end of the 1870s George H. Hoyt, aiming to emulate his success, invented Wheatena, possibly the oldest breakfast cereal still marketed under its original name. Hoyt and his successor Frank Fuller are credited with an important marketing idea: unlike oatmeal and other potential competitors, Wheatena was sold not from the sack but in brightly packaged boxes. Shoppers loved them.

Among the patients at Jackson's sanatorium was Ellen G. White. She went on to found the Seventh Day Adventist sect and to imbue it with her vegetarian beliefs. Her convert John Harvey Kellogg, who ran a sanatorium at Battle Creek, Michigan, began to develop cereal foods as part of the bland and meatless diet on which he famously insisted. It was in 1894 that Kellogg, as the result of an experiment that went wrong, invented wheat flakes, but his brother Will Keith Kellogg was the real history maker, not only because he applied the same process to maize – thus inventing Corn Flakes – but because he added sugar to them. Not a lot of sugar, but it was enough to disgust his brother and it was enough to sell his product to a mass market.

He went on to vastly enlarge this market with clever publicity: 'For thirty days please stop eating toasted corn flakes!' was one of his requests to a gullible public. 'Wink at your grocer and get a free box' was another temptation. The British author Saki (H. H. Munro) pointedly satirized such trickery in his short story 'Filboid Studge' (this being the clever new name destined to change the fortunes of the hitherto unsuccessful Pipenta).

One huge sombre poster depicted the Damned in Hell suffering a new torment from their inability to get at the Filboid Studge which elegant young fiends held in transparent bowls just beyond their reach . . . A single grim statement ran in bold letters along its base: 'They cannot buy it now.'

Kellogg's Corn Flakes
advertisement, 1906,
complete with grocer's
apostrophes.

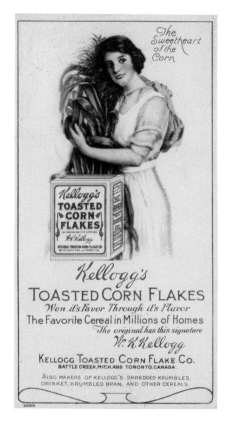

Free picture books and other bonuses, a long series of mascots calculated to catch a child's eye and a genre of unforgettable catchwords set the style for cereal publicity in the twentieth century. There's 'an arousing bunching and snapping to a bowl of breakfast cereal', writes Diane Ackerman in *A Natural History of the Senses*. So there is: a snap, crackle and pop, to be precise, and the marketers of Rice Krispies noticed it before she did. There's a strangely springy, loofah-like texture to Shredded Wheat, the extruded and baked cereal invented by the chronic diarrhoea sufferer Henry Perky in 1893. To a British audience every piece of Shredded Wheat embodies a challenge: natural and healthy as these remarkable constructions may be, surely no one can eat three of them?

The original earnest nineteenth-century insistence on the health benefit of cereal foods to every consumer has increasingly been frosted with an appeal to parents to consider their children's health. Saki faithfully recorded this trend: 'Once the womenfolk discovered that it was thoroughly unpalatable, their zeal in forcing it on their households knew no bounds.' Even Saki failed to foresee a further development, the gradual addition of larger quantities of sugar, which was to seduce the palates of these households and render 'force' unnecessary.

Even as sugar has increased and fibre has decreased, guilt-ridden mothers have been successfully persuaded that named breakfast cereals are essential to the building of healthy, strong children. Some names, for whatever combination of reasons, never become known beyond a national market, but Kellogg's products have always held a leading position worldwide, currently shared by those of Nestlé and a few others. Muesli and related products, originated by Maximilian Bircher-Benner at the beginning of the twentieth century and consisting of various combinations of rolled oats, dried fruit and nuts to be mixed with milk, are sold alongside the American-style cereals to a smaller, more self-

Women at the Kellogg's factory inspecting filled boxes of cereal before the boxes are sealed, 1934.

A. & C. Kaufmann, *Déjeuner à trois* (*The Breakfast*), *c.* 1873, chromolithograph.

conscious market with an equally sweet tooth. Across the world, even where adults continue to breakfast on local and traditional foods, sugary cereals are bought for children in greater quantities every year, and every year (even if the milk added to those cereals is the 'bluish' skimmed milk of Kingsley Amis's *Lucky Jim*) the children get fatter.

That same self-conscious market somehow continues to enjoy its meaty breakfasts now and then: as a weekend indulgence; as one way of getting value from a bed-and-breakfast package; or as a simple, sensuous luxury, the kind that was gently depicted not so long ago in Armistead Maupin's *Tales of the City*. As one scene opens, Michael is 'serving Mona breakfast in bed: poached eggs, nine-grain toast, Italian roast coffee and French sausages from Marcel & Henri'.

Service and Status, Poverty and Wealth

Breakfast is prepared and served – and that is not always the *mot juste* – faster and less formally than other meals. If grace is said, it is a shorter grace. Falstaff warned us of this, as already quoted: 'Grace thou wilt have none . . . not so much as will serve to be prologue to an egg and butter.' James Boswell recalled a conversation with Samuel Johnson 'about saying grace at breakfast (as we do in Scotland), as well as at dinner and supper'. Johnson thought it unnecessary, and Boswell, adding his private opinion in a footnote ('I think grace as proper at breakfast as at any other meal. It is the pleasantest meal we have') was evidently conscious that his English readership might take some persuading.

In the comfortable lodgings depicted in Oliver Wendell Holmes's *The Professor at the Breakfast-table* it is reasonable and normal that the lodgers help themselves to breakfast:

I fixed my eyes on a certain divinity-student, with the intention of exchanging a few phrases, and then forcing my court-card, namely, The great end of being. 'I will thank you for the sugar,' I said. 'Man is a dependent creature.'

'It is a small favor to ask,' said the divinity-student, and passed the sugar to me.

At Sandhurst Military Academy in the nineteenth century, as described by Edward Spencer Mott, breakfasts are good but they need no service. The 'board' is accessible to the breakfasters themselves, the beef is ready sliced, even the coffee is milked and sugared:

Breakfast was invariably served in the dining-halls, one to each company, in messes, and consisted of coffee (ready made, with milk and sugar added *à la* a charity-school treat), poured into slop-basins, and drunk out of them; bread-and-butter *à discretion*, and either eggs, cold boiled beef (ready cut), or sausages. Every item was excellent, and not much remained on the board after the mess had finished.

The best breakfasts, no doubt, are those occasional ones over which someone has taken particular care. Such is the breakfast in *Lady Chatterley's Lover* that Mellors sets on the bed for Connie to eat while 'he sat on the one chair, with his plate on his knees'. Such is the breakfast in

James Joyce's *Ulysses* that Leopold Bloom prepares for Molly, who is still in bed. His thoughts meanwhile linger partly on his own breakfast, probably kidneys, which he is about to go out and get. He has plenty of attention for the cat and her saucer of milk, but Molly's breakfast will still be exactly as she likes it. 'Another slice of bread and butter: three, four: right. She didn't like her plate full. Right. He turned from the tray, lifted the kettle off the hob and set it sideways on the fire. It sat there, dull and squat, its spout stuck out. Cup of tea soon. Good.' Thus the breakfast is completed and placed on the tray. As he carries it up the stairs he wonders, might she want kidneys too?

> She might like something tasty. Thin bread and butter she
> likes in the morning. Still perhaps: once in a way. He said softly
> in the bare hall:
> – I'm going round the corner. Be back in a minute.
> And when he had heard his voice say it he added:
> – You don't want anything for breakfast?
> A sleepy soft grunt answered:
> – Mn.

Even in less intimate circumstances we approve of breakfasts into which a little thought has gone, like those that John Beames and his fellow students enjoyed at Haileybury in 1856:

> We found . . . on the tongs, artfully stuck in between the bars
> of the grate to keep it hot, a mutton-chop or a curried sole or
> something of the kind. Breakfast parties were a favourite thing,
> and at these there were all sorts of luxuries provided by the
> students, and generally tankards of beer or claret.

The worst breakfasts are the formal and impersonal ones including, at one end of the scale, those that are formally served. We sympathize with Edward Spencer Mott's view that the breakfasts at late nineteenth-century Eton were no better for the fag-masters ('lords and masters') than the unlucky fags ('bondsmen') who were compelled to serve them:

In the first place, during the early hours of the day the inferior youth stood a very fair chance of being starved. Early school over, he had to prepare his lord and master's breakfast, occasionally a most elaborate meal. In a large kitchen, assisted by a cookmaid or two, the hereditary bondsmen exercised their talents at boiling, toasting, and frying. Tea or coffee – sometimes both – had to be made; muffins, sausages, bloaters, and bread toasted; ham and eggs fried; beef or ham scraped.

The unfortunate bondsmen 'had to wait at table until suffered to depart', Mott continues, but no Etonian table counted as many waiters as are visible in Diana Cooper's early twentieth-century reminiscence, in *The Light of Common Day*, of a ducal breakfast at nine o'clock: 'There are five men to wait on us, one for each. Everyone has their own tea or coffee pot. You help yourself to eggs and bacon . . . Herbrand eats a prodigious number of spring onions.' The spring onions we dismiss as a mere picturesque aristocratic eccentricity, but five men to wait at breakfast? And the diners still helped themselves to eggs and bacon? What were the five waiters doing? It is a little more reasonable that Prince von Pückler-Muskau, after describing the 'distinct apartment' of the housekeeper in an early nineteenth-century English country house, notes the adjoining room 'where coffee is made, and the store-room containing everything requisite for breakfast, which important meal, in England, belongs specially to her department'.

At the other end of the scale, and equally unpleasant, are the breakfasts about which no one cares. Those of the Paris hospital in George Orwell's essay 'How the Poor Die' ('At eight breakfast arrived, called army-fashion *la soupe*. It was soup, too, a thin vegetable soup with slimy hunks of bread floating about in it') and of the workhouse in 'The Spike' ('It was the invariable spike meal, always the same, whether breakfast, dinner or supper – half a pound of bread, a bit of margarine, and a pint of so-called tea. It took us five minutes to gulp down the cheap, noxious food') are worse even than those of the Burmese prison in his 'A Hanging' ('The convicts . . . were already receiving their breakfast. They squatted in long rows, each man holding a tin pannikin, while two warders with buckets marched round ladling out rice; it seemed quite

Advertisement for Scotch
Oats, British, 1899, with
a hint of disdain for the
non-porridge-eating
English.

a homely, jolly scene, after the hanging'). Orwell revelled in bad
breakfasts – remember the 'solid breakfasts', without a favourable adjective to redeem them, that were a defining feature of 'England, Your
England' – but these Orwellian breakfasts are scarcely worse than the
school meal in Charlotte Brontë's *Jane Eyre*:

> The classes were marshalled and marched into another room
> to breakfast: how glad I was to behold a prospect of getting
> something to eat! I was now nearly sick from inanition, having
> taken so little the day before.
>
> The refectory was a great, low-ceiled, gloomy room; on two
> long tables smoked basins of something hot, which, however,
> to my dismay, sent forth an odour far from inviting. I saw a
> universal manifestation of discontent when the fumes of the

repast met the nostrils of those destined to swallow it; from the van of the procession, the tall girls of the first class, rose the whispered words –

'Disgusting! The porridge is burnt again!'

'Silence!' ejaculated a voice . . . A long grace was said and a hymn sung; then a servant brought in some tea for the teachers, and the meal began.

Ravenous, and now very faint, I devoured a spoonful or two of my portion without thinking of its taste; but the first edge of hunger blunted, I perceived I had got in hand a nauseous mess; burnt porridge is almost as bad as rotten potatoes; famine itself soon sickens over it. The spoons were moved slowly: I saw each girl taste her food and try to swallow it; but in most cases the effort was soon relinquished. Breakfast was over, and none had breakfasted . . . I was one of the last to go out, and in passing the tables, I saw one teacher take a basin of the porridge and taste it; she looked at the others; all their countenances expressed displeasure, and one of them, the stout one, whispered –

'Abominable stuff! How shameful!'

Number-crunching

Enthusiasts of *The Lord of the Rings* are not alone in perceiving seven meals a day as the full quotient. The same conclusion was reached by Geoffrey Warren and his fellow researchers when they investigated British meals on a statistical basis, in the greatest detail that has ever been attempted, for the survey *The Foods We Eat* commissioned by W. S. Crawford Ltd (biscuit manufacturers) in 1958. Very much like Hobbits, the British of the 1950s were discovered to take as many as three meals before midday: Warren calls them 'Early Morning Tea', 'The British Breakfast' – we notice that even a sociological survey was compelled to emphasize the patriotic credentials of this particular meal – and 'The Mid-morning Break'.

Britain's national beverage at that date, and not only when taking Early Morning Tea, was tea. Average consumption across the whole country was nearly six cups per person per day. But the survey aimed to go into far greater detail than this. Investigators chose 4,557 over-sixteens to interview during a hot summer week of 1956, and another 4,557 of them, with similar demographic profile, in a cold winter week of 1957. What did these people eat and drink, and when?

First, Early Morning Tea. It transpired that just under half the population really took it: 40 per cent of men even in summer, and as many as 49 per cent of women in winter. Most of them took it between 6.30 and 8.30; on Saturdays it slipped to between 7.00 and 9.00, and on winter Sundays even after 9.00, almost as late in the day as Gargantua's breakfast. No surprise there. What would be interesting to know is whether this 40 per cent of English adults had anything to eat alongside their Early Morning Tea, but this the researchers didn't ask, or at least didn't record. We therefore don't know, statistically, whether or not the British in summer 1956 and winter 1957 were starting the day with a 'mouth-cleansing' tea-and-bread-and-butter, just like the ancient Egyptian and medieval European bread-and-wine.

Second, then, The British Breakfast. It was found that most of those who took Early Morning Tea took this second meal as well: around 40 per cent took both meals, nearly all the rest taking breakfast only. Of the whole sample, the number who breakfasted was over 90 per cent, and breakfast was eaten between about 7.00 and 10.00, men and women, summer and winter. On Sundays, though, the timetable slipped significantly: few began to eat before 8.00, and about a third were breakfasting at some unresearched hour after 9.30. What did they eat? We'll come back to that.

The numbers taking a Mid-morning Break were rather larger than those indulging in Early Morning Tea – about 52 per cent, significantly more in winter than in summer and slightly more women than men. Now this is where Warren and his researchers missed a trick. They didn't ask, or didn't write down, how many of those who took Early Morning Tea also in due course had a Mid-morning Break, and how many only took one or the other. Infuriatingly, therefore, we don't know at the end of the day whether nearly all the British of the 1950s were like the Hobbits of Tolkien's canonical text (two meals before midday for a total of six) or whether about half the British of this period were like the Hobbits of Peter Jackson's film (three meals before midday, a total of seven). Either is equally possible. What we do know, at least, is that the main constituent of the Mid-morning Break was tea (for roughly one-third of the total sample) or coffee (for roughly one-sixth). Other drinks were also-rans, and only about a quarter would indulge in a biscuit, bread and cheese, or something else solid at mid-morning.

Now, as promised, the big question: what did the British have for breakfast? Their choice of beverage is easy to state: it's tea again, for more than 85 per cent of the total sample. It has to be tea in order to account for the six cups of tea that each British person was drinking every day. Fewer than 5 per cent of the total sample had coffee at breakfast time, and about 5 per cent drank nothing at all.

As to the food, the survey distinguishes four possible courses, listed as: cereal/porridge; a cooked course; bread or toast; and fruit or fruit juice. The last option can be gently set aside, as can the small number of breakfasters who ate something that didn't fit into any of the categories: these groups together amount to less than 10 per cent of the total sample. For the rest, two came out on top. The most popular choice was the bread or toast course (with which we may assume butter or margarine) taken by between 50 per cent and 60 per cent of the total, winter and summer, men and women, though somewhat fewer of them on Sundays. Which may seem odd: keep it in mind. Marmalade was a luxury enjoyed by 25 per cent of the total; jam and honey were nowhere. Then the cooked course, which was taken by a far more variable proportion of the sample: only 37 per cent of women in summer, up to 60 per cent of men in winter; only 43 per cent of the total on summer weekdays, and up to 70 per cent of the total on winter Sundays. Those taking cereal were nearly 20 per cent, those taking porridge were very few in summer and up to 17 per cent in winter (but fewer on Sundays). The whole thing only works if the majority only took one of these courses, and the remainder at the very most two; and the answer to the unexpected Sunday result more or less proves this. The cooked breakfast on Sundays, a weekly luxury, tended to be an alternative to cereals and toast, not an addition to them. And what was the cooked breakfast? Twenty per cent to 40 per cent fried egg, 20 per cent to 45 per cent bacon, 8 per cent fried bread, 8 per cent boiled egg, about 6 per

Porridge in a very small glass bowl, to be compared to the rice porridge seen on p. 164.

cent tomatoes and that's it . . . except that as many as 8 per cent allowed themselves a sausage on a winter Sunday.

The result of these statistics, if we compare them with what we know from history and literature, is this. The typical 1950s British breakfast was a cooked breakfast, but with only one, or at the most two, cooked items from a very limited range; plus bread, plus tea. A Sunday cooked breakfast was even more popular than the weekday cooked breakfast; it arrived a little later in the morning and would probably amount to two, possibly even three, cooked items. Breakfast cereals, though assiduously marketed for decades, had not yet invaded the majority of households. But they were on the increase.

Devilled lamb's kidneys on toast.

five

Feeling for
Breakfast

As Bloomsday begins, the hero of Joyce's *Ulysses* has his mind on breakfast. Bloom habitually 'ate with relish the inner organs of beasts and fowls. He liked thick giblet soup, nutty gizzards, a stuffed roast heart, liverslices fried with crustcrumbs, fried hencods' roes. Most of all he liked grilled mutton kidneys which gave to his palate a fine tang of faintly scented urine.' Some time will pass before this morning's wish is fulfilled. First, as already quoted, he has to prepare Molly's breakfast and the cat's breakfast. Over both of these tasks he takes appropriately loving care (the cat is the more vocal of the two in its gratitude). Then he can give full attention to his own breakfast, which requires an outing to the butcher's. 'He halted before Dlugacz's window, staring at the hanks of sausages, polonies, black and white . . . The shiny links, packed with forcemeat, fed his gaze and he breathed in tranquilly the lukewarm breath of cooked spicy pigs' blood. A kidney oozed bloodgouts on the willowpatterned dish: the last', and Bloom knows at once, as if he had not known long before, which of these constituents of a meaty Irish breakfast he will choose today.

He takes his place inside, but the next-door girl is there first: will she buy it before him? 'And a pound and a half of Denny's sausages,' she reads from her list, while Bloom's eyes rest on her vigorous hips. 'The ferreteyed porkbutcher folded the sausages he had snipped off with blotchy fingers, sausagepink. Sound meat there: like a stallfed heifer,' Bloom thinks, his mind still on the next-door girl. '"Thank you, my miss. And one shilling threepence change. For you, please?" Mr Bloom pointed quickly. To catch up and walk behind her if she went slowly, behind her moving hams. Pleasant to see first thing in the morning. Hurry up, damn it . . . "Threepence, please." His hand accepted the moist tender gland and slid it into a sidepocket.' Too late: she has disappeared. His consolation is the kidney, which is now his. In all of literature there are few more sustained interweavings of gastronomy and sensuality; there is perhaps only one exploration of the consciousness of a single would-be breakfaster that is fuller than this.

Its Construction

As we saw, Plutarch was the earliest writer to perceive the big distinction between breakfast and other meals. People breakfast 'without any great trouble', with whatever food is at hand; they take breakfast wherever they are – Apuleius' narrator and his companion under a plane tree, Don Quixote and Sancho beside a clear and limpid spring in a shady clump of trees. At the Joads' farm in Oklahoma there's not enough room around the table, which would be a disaster at any literary lunch or dinner but is almost normal at breakfast time: 'Jus' get yaself a plate an' set down wherever ya can. Out in the yard or someplace.' One can of course take breakfast in bed. One can do that even in company, as Evelina was shocked to realize in Fanny Burney's *Evelina*: 'I found Madame Duval at breakfast in bed, though Monsieur Du Bois was in the chamber; which so much astonished me, that I was, involuntarily, retiring . . . She has a very bad cold, and Monsieur Du Bois is so hoarse, he can hardly speak.' Might Evelina have stumbled upon evidence that Madame Duval and Monsieur Du Bois were close to one another even before breakfast time? Breakfast in bed may have one, or two, or more than two participants: in Madame Duval's case there are three if we include the observer Fanny, while in the case of Mellors and Lady Chatterley there are three only if we include the omniscient narrator.

It seems that breakfast is prepared by whoever is free. Thus with our very first breakfast, the one in Eumaios' hut, the wandering beggar helps to prepare it; with our second, that on the shore of the Sea of Tiberias, the stranger prepares it; in our third, at the keeper's lodge in Fressingfield, the visitors will put up with food 'such as poor keepers have within their lodge', though they suspect that Margaret 'speaks least, to hold her

Charles Burton Barber, *Suspense*, 1894, oil on canvas.

promise sure', in other words, that she will provide more than she has dared to promise in advance. At the Joads' the preparing and timing of breakfast depends simply on Ma, who will 'yell breakfast in a minute'. She has salt pork for everybody but claims that it's 'jus' lucky I made plenty bread this morning.'

Whoever does the preparation, people must finally make their breakfasts for themselves. The adventurous *Times* correspondent G. E. Morrison, in his 1895 memoir *An Australian in China*, admitted with bluff honesty that he had failed to do this, supplying at the same time a character sketch of his stolid attendant Laohwan:

> Long before daybreak he was about again, attending to the mule and preparing my porridge and eggs for breakfast. He thought

I liked my eggs hard, and each morning construed my look of remonstrance into one of approbation. It is very true of the Chinaman that precedent determines his action. The first morning Laohwan boiled the eggs hard and I could not reprove him. Afterwards of course he made a point of serving me the eggs every morning in the same way. I could say in Chinese 'I don't like them,' but the morning I said so Laohwan applied my dislike to the eggs, not to their condition of cooking, and saying in Chinese 'Good, good,' he obligingly ate them for me.

Thomas Forester in his travels in Norway in 1848 was more successful at making his breakfast for himself. 'It is highly expedient that travellers in such a country should be able to make a very early and substantial breakfast; for, beyond what their wallets may contain, and a chance bowl of milk by the way, there is little hope of their meeting with any refreshment till nightfall . . . Rashers and steaks, and such relishes' are not available and, Forester continues, seemed to belong to another world. In their place:

Rice porridge (*juk* in Cantonese, congee in English) with boiled quails' eggs.

they call it grod, but it is probably well known to many of my readers under the familiar names of oatmeal-porridge, or stir-about . . . To the traveller it is invaluable; to the man of sedentary habits, bilious, dyspeptic, a prey to all the ills which a town life entails on the human system, its adoption will afford more relief than the best prescription of his physician.

Forester goes on to explain how this wonderful substance is cooked – his recipe was quoted in chapter Three – and how it is to be converted into a complete and satisfying breakfast for the traveller. 'Add only a slice of rye-bread, or, if that cannot be procured, of a wheaten loaf made of flour from which no part of the bran has been extracted, and the practice will do more for his health than all the drugs of the chemist,' he advises, allowing his mind to rest briefly on his readers' lower digestive tracts; then, as an afterthought, he admits how he actually managed to swallow all this porridge. 'Sometimes we added cream, for in the pastoral districts we made unscrupulous use of the bowls of cream with which we were every where supplied; our own stores furnished the sugar.' Thus, like a twenty-first-century hotel guest at a breakfast buffet, Forester took the ingredients that came to hand and constructed his breakfast for himself.

Its Importance

In *Breakfast at Tiffany's*, Truman Capote's novella of 1958, there is no breakfast beyond the title metaphor (though the film version, taking its title with due seriousness, begins with breakfast). In *Breakfast on Pluto*, the novel by Patrick McCabe of 1998 and film adaptation of 2005, breakfast is again a metaphor, barely visible in these lines quoted from the screenplay:

> PATRICK: . . . all the songs she'd listened to, all the love songs, that they were only songs.
> BERTIE: What's wrong with that?
> PATRICK: Nothing, if you don't believe in them. But she did, you see. She believed in enchanted evenings, and she believed that

a small cloud passed overhead and cried down on a flower
bed, and she even believed there was breakfast to be had –
BERTIE: Where?
PATRICK: On Pluto. The mysterious, icy wastes of Pluto.

Laurence Sterne delivers his chapter on breakfasts in volume VIII
of *Tristram Shandy*, and for him, too, breakfast is a metaphor. We are
in the throes of the love affair between widow Wadman and uncle
Toby Shandy. As yet uncle Toby does not love widow Wadman. She has
two choices, therefore: to love him anyway, or not to love him. 'Widow
Wadman would do neither the one or the other – Gracious heaven!'
Tristram exclaims, and immediately confesses to his own indecision in
similar cases:

> Whenever it so falls out, which it sometimes does about the
> equinoxes, that an earthly goddess is so much this, and that,
> and t'other, that I cannot eat my breakfast for her – and that
> she careth not three halfpence whether I eat my breakfast or
> no –
>   – Curse on her! and so I send her to Tartary.

He changes his mind, brings her back again, curses her again and
swears to have no more of it. 'It' changes from woman to love to sex in
every clause, and the current metaphor for it changes just as frequently:

> No; I shall never have a finger in the pie . . .
> Crust and crumb
> Inside and out
> Top and bottom – I detest it, I hate it, I repudiate it –
>   I'm sick at the sight of it –
> 'Tis all pepper,
> garlick,
> staragen,
> salt, and
> devil's dung – by the great arch-cook of cooks, who does
> nothing, I think, from morning to night, but sit down by the

fire-side and invent inflammatory dishes for us, I would not touch it for the world –

– O Tristram! Tristram! cried Jenny.

The finger in the pie brings the imagery back to food. 'Crust and crumb' is the old phrase – bread, the indispensable, the breakfast staple – already familiar in Sterne's time from its use in *King Lear*. And then the salty and musky tastes that he will have no more of: staragen is tarragon, which one can easily have too much of, and the same can be said of garlic and pepper; devil's dung is asafoetida, more repulsive than the others yet culinary and salutary; and it is from the mention of this that the arch-cook of cooks comes into Tristram's mind. But the sequence began with breakfast.

Breakfast, to those who can take it less emotionally, may quite simply be what one gets out of the way before the real work of the day begins – and then forgets about. In the analysis of mealtimes in the Hippocratic text *Ancient Medicine*, quoted in chapter One, breakfast is not even mentioned. A light meal taken at dawn or soon after was called *akratisma*, but the fact that the author does not even mention it suggests that he did not count it as a meal. This may seem strange, but exactly the same view is taken by some anthropologists, who are prepared to argue that since meals are social events and breakfast is not (always) a social event, breakfast is not a meal. Nor are they alone. The historian Robert Latham, editor of Pepys's *Diaries*, in the course of claiming that the diarist usually did not take breakfast, writes flatly: 'Pepys may well have had a drink and a bite of bread on rising which go unnoticed in the diary. But not a meal.'

'If you sing before breakfast, you'll cry before night', some have been warned. 'Hope is a good breakfast but a poor supper', and, perhaps more usefully, 'Pride often breakfasts with plenty, dines with poverty, and sups with infamy.' The anonymous author of *The Family Book, or Instructions Concerning all the Relations of Life* ascribes this last sententious utterance to a neighbour, 'good Mr Sutton', and who are we to doubt him? The point of it, among the rest of Mr Sutton's 'advice to young tradesmen', is that you should not reject potential business whatever its source: you may have enough money to buy your breakfast, but bankruptcy – which means infamy – will follow if you don't get out there and make more. Not dissimilar is the phrase thus recorded in the 1871 edition of Brewer's *Dictionary of Phrase and Fable*: "'Disorder,'" says Benjamin Franklin, "breakfasts with Plenty, dines with Poverty, sups with Misery, and sleeps with Death.'" Behave yourself, in other words, keep to an orderly timetable and, as before, breakfast lightly. Franklin may have said it, but notice that Brewer vouches for this, not I. The general trend of these proverbs, as far as breakfast is concerned, is that breakfast doesn't count for much.

It counts to some – to the 'condemned man', for example, who famously 'ate a hearty breakfast'. These words, which I cannot trace earlier than their use by A. Bertram Chandler in his story 'Last Day' of 1953 (and by that time they were already a cliché) are a reworking of the thought expressed 2,500 years ago by King Leonidas of Sparta. Or so it is claimed. Here is another quotation that may well be apocryphal. With his 600 Spartan warriors it was Leonidas' fate to defend the narrow pass of Thermopylai against the vast Persian army in the year 490 BC. His exhortation to his troops is not quoted by any early sources. How could it be, since he and every man who heard his words was killed that very day? But Roman authors, some 500 years after the event, were quite certain that they knew what Leonidas said: *Sic prandete, conmilitones, tamquam apud inferos cenaturi*. In plain English, he told his fellow soldiers to breakfast like men who would be dining in hell. The Greek word is *ariston*, the Latin *prandium*, and since the Spartans are awaiting imminent enemy attack and the Persians are surrounding them at dawn we know how to translate these words: this is not lunch, this is the condemned man's hearty breakfast.

Others see every breakfast as important, not only one's last. A certain young Scotswoman, urged by her friends to marry a man with no money ('Marry for love and work for siller') wisely replied, 'It's a' vera true, but a kiss and a tinniefu' o' could water maks a gey wersh breakfast'. The saying appears in 1861 in E. B. Ramsay's *Reminiscences of Scottish Life and Character*, and the girl certainly meant not only that it is better to kiss men with money but also that a breakfast, if it is *wersh*, 'weak, un-nourishing', fails to fulfil the true end of a breakfast. Dr Folliott in Thomas Love Peacock's *Crotchet Castle*, before beginning to discuss

Breakfast in the trenches, 1914.

the constituents of a perfect breakfast as quoted in chapter two, gives a few words to the importance of breakfast in general: 'You are a man of taste, Mr Crotchet. A man of taste is seen at once in the array of his breakfast-table. It is the foot of Hercules.' Pythagoras, they say, calculated the size of the Greek hero Herakles' foot from the unusual length of the racetrack at Olympia which he was said to have paced out; then, having shown the length of his foot, he calculated the height of Herakles. Breakfast is the measure of the day, just as the foot is the measure of Herakles.

It's safe to say that only Thomas Love Peacock would have likened a breakfast to Herakles' foot. Many others, though, ever since his time, have taken up Dr Folliott's claim that breakfast has a special significance. 'The breakfast is a very important meal,' wrote Edward Playter in *Elementary Anatomy, Physiology and Hygiene* (1879). That was already very close to the modern cliché, but the first writer to claim in so many words that it is 'the most important meal of the day' may possibly have been M. T. Colbrath in *What to Get for Breakfast* (1882). The same claim is made with greater confidence in *The Art of Living in Australia* (1893) by Philip Muskett who insists that time must be given to this essential meal if dyspepsia is not to follow:

American poster, 1941–3. Americans, newly at war, were the target of government health and nutrition campaigns.

How very much better than all this bustle, hurry, and scuttle an hour's earlier rising would be! It would afford ample time for the bath, which should be a bath in the truest sense of the term; it would, above all, give a proper opportunity for a leisurely breakfast, which is in every respect the most important meal of the day; and lastly, it would save that wild dash at the last, which is so fatal to proper digestion and well-being.

These are all practical books. The commonplace had reached everyday life – and therefore fiction – by 1896 when the Scottish–Canadian author Robert Barr, in *A Woman Intervenes*, depicted a father urging his son out of bed with the words: 'Get up! get up! breakfast, my boy! Breakfast! – the most important meal in the day to a healthy man.'

Its Discomforts

It may be 'an important meal'; it may – for who could possibly disprove it? – be 'the most important meal'; but it is a difficult meal, and never more difficult than in the Australian novels of Henry Handel Richardson. These trace with surgical precision the difficulties of a family not unlike hers, and the tragic decline of a father. The second volume in the trilogy, *The Way Home* (1925), shows the frustrations of house guests at unfamiliar breakfast routines. Curiously similar feelings are evoked in heroines of late eighteenth- and early nineteenth-century novels who find themselves breakfasting as house guests – Fanny Burney's *Evelina*, Grace Nugent of Maria Edgeworth's *The Absentee*, Fanny Price of Jane Austen's *Mansfield Park*; is it a coincidence that all four authors are women? But Richardson (Ethel Florence Lindesay Richardson to give her real name) drives home the discomfort. Richard Mahony has brought his family back to Australia and they are temporarily staying with the Devines. Ten o'clock has struck, but Mary is still in bedgown and slippers, though she has been up for a couple of hours. It was 'one of the rules of this extraordinary house that visitors did not breakfast till after ten; the longer after, the better, but at any moment *past* the hour'. The servants were required to 'hover perpetually alert for the ringing of the dining-room bell':

> Many and scathing were Richard's comments on the prac-
> tice of using your guests as the stick with which to belabour
> your slaves . . . The first morning he and Mary had blun-
> dered in this respect; on the second they were wiser; and now
> loitered chilly and hungry above-stairs . . . Breakfast coped
> with, Mary waited, dressed for driving, for the carriage to
> come round, and for her hostess to cease goading on her
> several maidservants.

Much later, in the third novel, *Ultima Thule*, as the family finances unravel and as Richard's mind shows increasing signs of disturbance, 'they were at breakfast when the summons came – breakfast, the hardest meal of any to get through without friction':

Richard invariably ate at top speed and with his eyes glued to his plate; in order, he said, not to be obliged to see Zara's dusty crepe and bombazine, the mere sight of which on these hot mornings took away his appetite . . . Zara had a patent habit of masticating each mouthful so-and-so many times before swallowing; and the children forgot to eat, in counting their aunt's bites. With their ears cocked for the click at the finish. Mamma said it was her teeth that did it, and it was rude to listen.

These are sad breakfasts, like those of the elderly Samuel Johnson as he described in a letter: 'When I rise, my breakfast is solitary; the black dog waits to share it.' *The black dog*, an expression familiar in Mrs Thrale's correspondence with Johnson and famously adopted by Winston Churchill, is melancholy.

Equally unhappy, though for a specific reason, is the English traveller Edward Waverley's Scottish breakfast in Sir Walter Scott's novel *Waverley*: 'Waverley sat down almost in silence, and with an air of absence and abstraction which could not give Miss Bradwardine a favourable opinion of his talents for conversation. He answered at random one or two observations . . .'. She soon gives up the attempt, unaware that Waverley has all the time been wondering whether he would have to fight a duel with his fellow guest Balmawhapple, a thought that might put any man off his breakfast. He sees Balmawhapple through the window, exits hastily, is greeted with an apology and returns in a calmer frame of mind to do

> much greater honour to the delicacies of Miss Bradwardine's breakfast-table than his commencement had promised. Balmawhapple, on the contrary, seemed embarrassed and dejected . . . To a question from Miss Bradwardine, he muttered in answer something about his horse having fallen; and seeming desirous to escape both from the subject and the company, he arose as soon as breakfast was over.

The hospitable Miss Bradwardine must certainly have wished she had not got up for breakfast that day. Fanny Price, the protagonist of

Jane Austen's *Mansfield Park*, published in the same year as *Waverley*, is encouraged to be lazy for a very similar reason (as quoted in chapter Four). She gets up for breakfast, none the less, to say goodbye to her brother William and to his friend Crawford with whom she is supposed to be in love.

> The breakfast was soon over . . . the last kiss was given, and William was gone . . . short and pleasant had been the meal. After seeing William to the last moment, Fanny walked back to the breakfast-room with a very saddened heart to grieve over the melancholy change; and there her uncle kindly left her to cry in peace, conceiving, perhaps, that the deserted chair of each young man might exercise her tender enthusiasm, and that the remaining cold pork bones and mustard in William's plate might but divide her feelings with the broken egg-shells in Mr Crawford's. She sat and cried *con amore* as her uncle intended, but it was *con amore* fraternal and no other. William was gone.

Sad or not, breakfasts have a habit of being silent. At the Joads' farm in Oklahoma 'there was no talk until the food was gone, the coffee drunk; only the crunch of chewed food and the slup of coffee cooled in transit to the tongue'. It may be imagined that the breakfasts of the Samsa household described in Franz Kafka's *Metamorphosis* were equally silent: breakfast for Gregor Samsa's father, who undoubtedly set the tone, was *die wichtigste Mahlzeit des Tages*, yes, 'the most important meal of the day', but this was not because of its ingredients but because 'by reading all the different newspapers he made it last for hours'. At Rodway's crowded coffee-house at Billingsgate in 1851 breakfast was 'so extremely silent that the smacking of lips and sipping of coffee were alone heard'.

Earlier, when Prince von Pückler-Muskau breakfasted in Ireland in 1828 with six or seven sturdy squires, he observed that 'they do not think much, but their life is all the more gay and careless'. He leaves us to guess whether not thinking much led to not speaking much. Much earlier still comes a medieval breakfast narrated in the Jerusalem Talmud

German breakfast, 1934, poster.

at which the only necessary words were spoken in advance of the meal and after it:

> Rabbi Abbahu says in the name of Rabbi Yohanan that there was once a man who wanted to join a breakfast. Another said to him: 'Will you give me what you owe me?' 'Yes,' he said. When they got up from their meal he said, 'I don't owe you anything.' The one who had invited him objected: 'I have witnesses to what you said.' He replied: 'I only said it so as not to spoil your breakfast.'

Conversation at breakfast is hard to handle for Catherine Morland in Jane Austen's *Northanger Abbey*. She was terrified by the storm in the night and wants to forget it, "'but we have a charming morning after it,'" she hazards, attempting a diversion; "'what beautiful hyacinths! I have just learnt to love a hyacinth." "And how might you learn?" the General asks sharply. "'By accident or argument?'" Even a throwaway word can start a moral debate at Northanger Abbey. She tries an escape route: praise of the crockery.

> It had been the General's choice. He was enchanted by her approbation of his taste, confessed it to be neat and simple, thought it right to encourage the manufacture of his country; and for his part, to his uncritical palate, the tea was as well flavoured from the clay of Staffordshire, as from that of Dresden. But this was quite an old set, purchased two years ago . . .

Catherine's defences are down, and the General takes this opporunity to strike: 'he trusted, however, that an opportunity might ere long occur of selecting one – though not for himself!' – with a sly hint at romance and forthcoming marriage and wedding presents.

Its Purposes

Given the right company breakfast may be a time for lively talk. Samuel Pepys's New Year breakfast in 1661 was shared with several of his family including his cousin Anthony Fenner, who might have been expected to send his excuses '(Anthony's only son dying this morning, yet he was so civil to come and was pretty merry)'. With wine and ale as beverages they 'were very merry till about 11 a-clock'. There was lively conversation, too, when Macaulay dined at Holland House in 1831:

> Our breakfast party consisted of my Lord and Lady, myself, Lord Russell, and Luttrell. You must have heard of Luttrell . . . Lady Holland told us her dreams; how she had dreamed that a mad dog bit her foot, and how she set off to Brodie, and lost her way in St Martin's Lane, and could not find him. She hoped, she said, the dream would not come true. I said that I had had a dream which admitted of no such hope; for I had dreamed

that I heard Pollock speak in the House of Commons, that the speech was very long, and that he was coughed down. This dream of mine diverted them much.

Can we say that breakfast, differing as it does from other meals, has a definable purpose of its own? In looking for an answer it is necessary to dismiss the 'business breakfasts' advertised to would-be tycoons who can imagine nothing better to do at breakfast than talk business, even planning to do so in advance. That's not what breakfast is for. It is advisable to glance back at the historical and literary breakfasts already quoted and to recall a feature quite generally shared among them: whatever their purpose may have seemed to be in advance, they transcended it. Breakfast exists to be unexpected. When Joseph Haydn, calling at Bonn on his way back from London to Vienna, was invited to breakfast by the electoral orchestra at Godesberg in July 1792, they expected to lionize him and he expected to be lionized. This happened, but what also happened is that he encountered the young Beethoven, was astonished by his work and persuaded him to set out for Vienna. A breakfast intended as a bland and relatively meaningless

Aristide Briand breakfasts with German ministers Joseph Wirth and Robert Schmidt, The Hague, January 1930.

occasion was in the event a turning point for Beethoven and a land-mark in musical history.

If we consult that infallible oracle, the World Wide Web, on the purpose of breakfast, we find repeated mentions (every one of them a slight misquotation) of an oracular statement on the subject by none other than Thomas Babington Macaulay. It was issued when Mac-aulay, now a grander and older man than the young MP who accepted Lord Holland's breakfast invitation, sat at breakfast with Harriet Beecher Stowe in around 1850. Here is what Stowe said (in *Sunny Memories of Foreign Lands*) that Macaulay really said:

> Looking around the table, and seeing how every body seemed to be enjoying themselves, I said to Macaulay, that these breakfast parties were a novelty to me; that we never had them in America, but that I thought them the most delightful form of social life.
>
> He seized upon the idea, as he often does, and turned it play-fully inside out, and shook it on all sides, just as one might play with the lustres of a chandelier – to see them glitter. He expatiated on the merits of breakfast parties as compared with all other parties. He said dinner parties are mere formalities. You invite a man to dinner because you must invite him; because you are acquainted with his grandfather, or it is proper you should; but you invite a man to breakfast because you want to see him. You may be sure, if you are invited to breakfast, there is some-thing agreeable about you.

There is no need to add that this last idea struck Harriet Beecher Stowe as 'very sensible'. Her fellow guests liked it too. As she observes, 'having the fact before our eyes that we were invited to breakfast', it would have been very odd if they hadn't liked it.

Henry James liked the idea too: he savoured the breakfasts to which he was invited in Half-Moon Street in 1870s London, relished the encounters, feared but surely never avoided the questionings that seemed to turn him into the object of enquiry ('only not perfectly ridicu-lous because perfectly insignificant') rather than the cool observer. In spite of this, the breakfast that is most fully experienced and described in James's memoir *The Middle Years* isn't any of these. It is his first meal in England, his breakfast on landing at Liverpool in 1870 'in the gusty, cloudy, overwhelmingly English morning'. This led him to 'a late breakfast in the coffee-room of the old Adelphi Hotel ("Radley's", as I had to deplore its lately having ceased to be dubbed)' and to miscellaneous sense-impressions:

> I observed for instance that in England the plate of buttered muffin and its cover were sacredly set upon the slop-bowl after hot water had been ingenuously poured into the same . . . I must have had with my tea and my muffin a boiled egg or two and a dab of marmalade, but it was from a far other store of condiments I most liberally helped myself . . . I was again and again in the aftertime to win back the homeliest notes of the impression, the damp and darksome light washed in from the steep, black, bricky street, the crackle of the strong draught of the British 'sea-coal' fire.

Even the 'truth to type' of the waiter impresses him, 'truth to history, to literature, to poetry, to Dickens'. With all this, the breakfast is pure and perfect to James: its literary function, after all, is to be itself.

The Perfect Breakfast

It is open to all men to choose their perfect breakfast. One choice is simply stated by the inconsequential Mr Skimpole in Dickens's *Bleak House*:

> This is my frugal breakfast. Some men want legs of beef and mutton for breakfast; I don't. Give me my peach, my cup of coffee, and my claret; I am content. I don't want them for themselves; they remind me of the sun. There's nothing solar about legs of beef and mutton. Mere animal satisfaction.

The meal that is taken in the first chapter of *Tom Brown's Schooldays* (1857), when the overnight coach stops at breakfast time at a pure and

Claude Monet, *Le Déjeuner*, 1868, oil on canvas.

perfect inn – '"Twenty minutes here, gentlemen," says the coachman, as they pull up at half-past seven at the inn-door' – is pure and perfect breakfast. It has no other function than to warm the reader who is as yet cold, to feed the reader who does not yet know where the next meal will be:

> the table covered with the whitest of cloths and of china, and bearing a pigeon-pie, ham, round of cold boiled beef cut from a mammoth ox, and the great loaf of household bread on a wooden trencher. And here comes in the stout head waiter, puffing under a tray of hot viands – kidneys and a steak, transparent rashers and poached eggs, buttered toast and muffins, coffee and tea, all smoking hot. The table can never hold it all. The cold meats are removed to the sideboard – they were only put on for show and to give us an appetite.

Anyone who has recently taken an overnight bus, say, from London to Cork, and stopped at Waterford for breakfast, will recognize the warmth and reassurance of this description, though tables and sideboards are not as heavily laden in twenty-first-century reality as they were in Thomas Hughes's nineteenth-century imagination.

Sir Thomas's breakfast as sketched by Thomas Ingoldsby (that is, Richard Barham, who wrote 'The Knight and the Lady' as one of his *Ingoldsby Legends* in 1843), has no other function than scene-setting and character painting:

> It seems he had taken
> A light breakfast – bacon,
> An egg – with a little broiled haddock – at most
> A round and a half of some hot butter'd-toast,
> With a slice of cold sirloin from yesterday's roast.
> And then – let me see! –
> He had two – perhaps three
> Cups (with sugar and cream) of strong Gunpowder tea,
> With a spoonful in each of some choice eau de vie,
> – Which with nine out of ten would perhaps disagree.

The Knight, excessively warmed perhaps by this 'light' and perfect breakfast, will go insect-hunting, will fall into a pond and drown, and the Lady, if she mourns him at all, will do so only very briefly.

The best of breakfasts at nineteenth-century inns – in Wales in George Borrow's *Wild Wales*, somewhere near Woburn in Prince von Pückler-Muskau's *Tour* – have the same function. Pückler-Muskau's reader is tempted to touch the 'large tea-urn, prettily surrounded by silver tea-canisters . . . and a milk-jug', to sample the 'inviting plate of boiled eggs, another *ditto* of broiled *oreilles de cochon à la Sainte Ménéhould*', to scent the 'muffins, kept warm by a hot water-plate', to taste the 'ham, flaky white bread, dry and buttered toast' and the 'best fresh butter in an elegant glass vessel', to sip the 'very good green and black tea' – all this for only 'two shillings (16 *Groschen*)'. Borrow's readers imagine them-selves before a 'noble breakfast' such as Borrow himself 'might have read of, but had never before seen. There was tea and coffee, a goodly white loaf and butter . . . a couple of eggs and two mutton chops . . . broiled and pickled salmon . . . fried trout . . . potted trout and potted shrimps', and they come away from the experience fuller and more satisfied.

But it is not the whole task of literature to reassure the reader. I estimated Leopold Bloom's breakfast, published in 1922 and quoted at the beginning of this chapter, to be the second fullest exploration of the consciousness of a single, solitary breakfaster. As a conclusion let me quote from the fullest of all, published twelve years later and, in its own way, even less reassuring. Through a French window the narrator sees a spectacle that affects him profoundly, commanding his whole attention. A parlour maid places a tray on a table:

> It was a well-laden tray. There was a coffee-pot on it, also toast in considerable quantity, and furthermore a covered dish. It was this last that touched the spot. Under that cover there might be eggs, there might be bacon, there might be sausages, there might be kidneys . . .
>
> I estimated that I had possibly fifty seconds for the stern task before me. Allow twenty for nipping in, three for snaffling the works, and another twenty-five for getting back into the bushes again . . .

The plan (as any reader of *Thank You, Jeeves* will have guessed) failed. While still in the room the narrator is surprised by footsteps, hides behind a desk and is trapped there, within sight and scent of his prey, by successive meetings of his enemies. He has time to make himself known to one sympathetic presence, and to reach out hungrily: '"You are proposing to eat his lordship's breakfast, sir?"' Indeed he was, if there were ever time.

'But I'm starving . . . Have you had breakfast, Jeeves?'
'Yes, sir.'
'What did you have?'
'The juice of an orange, sir, followed by Cute Crispies – an American cereal – scrambled eggs with a slice of bacon, and toast and marmalade.'
'Oh, gosh! The whole washed down, no doubt, with a cup of strengthening coffee?'
'Yes, sir.'
'Oh, my God! You really don't think I could just sneak a single sausage?'

More footsteps, and this time the new visitor fails to resist the identical temptation. The sounds are heard of coffee being poured, of the domed cover being lifted. 'It was the scent of kippered herrings that was now wafted to me like a benediction . . . I could mark every mouthful and each in turn went through me like a knife.' More meetings; discussion, even, of whether others less deserving need breakfast. A cup of coffee and ham sandwich will be delivered to a distant recipient, and the narrator, emptier than ever, winces as he hears it. Among these discussions a plan is formed, and Bertie Wooster, revealed at last, is constrained to play the leading role in it.

'But one word. When I come out, do I get breakfast?'
'You get the best breakfast Chuffnell Hall can provide.'
I eyed him searchingly.
'Kippers?'
'Schools of kippers.'

Samuel D. Ehrhart, man testing cereal, from *Some Deserving Candidates for the Hero Fund*, 1904.

> 'Toast?'
> 'Mounds of toast.'
> 'And coffee?'
> 'Pots.'

Bertie consents, all is resolved, and the following chapter tells briefly of his reward, or rather of the evidence it has left behind. In that last scene the late morning sunlight falls 'on the skeletons of four kippered herrings; on a coffee-pot; and on an empty toast-rack'.

James Gillray, 'Matrimonial-Harmonics', *c.* 1805, colour engraving. Breakfast depicted in a series of satires on marriage. He has tired of music, she hasn't. The baby interests no one. Love, modelled in china on the mantelpiece, is dead.

Epilogue:
Damer's Muffins

The unfortunate John Damer is remembered for nothing at all in this world except his spendthrift existence, his dramatic end and two breakfasts.

Born in 1743, he was the eldest of the three sons of Joseph Damer, a rich financier, remarkably ambitious and, according to those who fell foul of him, unusually unpleasant. His three sons milked London for its pleasures in the early 1770s, trading on the apparent fact that when their father died they would be rich. They were wrong: he was spending it all on his future peerage (he died Earl of Dorchester) and on his great houses, Milton Abbey in Dorset and the Park Lane mansion that was to become the Dorchester.

Young John Damer's first famous breakfast was on the occasion on which he paid a morning visit to the economist Adam Smith. Now this is an absent-minded-professor story, not a Damer story: all we learn from it about John Damer is that he had an interest in political economy that we would otherwise not have guessed. As to Adam Smith, Mary Coke's diary makes it clear that he was interested in economics to the exclusion of all else:

> Mr Damer made him a visit the other morning as he was going to breakfast, and falling into discourse, Mr Smith took a piece of bread and butter, which after he had rolled round and round, he put into the teapot, and when he had tasted it, he said it was the worst tea he had ever met with. Mr Damer told him he did not in the least doubt it, for that he had

made it of the bread and butter he had been rolling about his finger.

That breakfast was in 1767, the same year in which John Damer married. Marriage, to the sculptor Anne Conway, did him no good at all. Her inclinations were for her own sex; his chosen pleasures were those of a bachelor and he pursued them with undiminished enthusiasm. Nine years later he found himself separated from his wife and £70,000 in debt. His father, to whom he made a final appeal, refused to help, and John decided that there was only one way out. Hence his second famous breakfast, dated 15 August 1776.

The story as it immediately emerged is told in a letter by Horace Walpole who, being Anne's cousin, was personally involved in the tragedy:

> On Thursday, Mr Damer supped at the Bedford Arms in Covent Garden, with four common women, a blind fiddler, and no other man. At three in the morning he dismissed his seraglio, bidding each receive her guinea at the bar, and ordering [the fiddler] to come up again in half an hour. When he returned he found a dead silence, and smelt gunpowder. He called, the master of the house came up, and found Mr Damer sitting in his chair, dead, with a pistol by his side and another in his pocket.

No breakfast as yet. Nor is there a breakfast in the laconic report of this suicide ('heir to 30,000*l*. a year, but of a turn rather too eccentric to be confined within the limits of any fortune. Coroner's verdict, "Lunacy,"') that appeared shortly afterwards in the *Gentleman's Magazine* with no indiscreet mention of John Damer's name. There is a supper, but no breakfast, in the unpublished minute of evidence to the coroner's jury, which names Damer himself alongside three witnesses, Richard Burnet the blind fiddler, John Robinson the landlord and the girl that Damer specially asked for, 'little Miss Richmond that sings'.

Three years later the story had grown. Against the date 16 April 1779 James Boswell reports a significant conversation, on the subject of suicide by shooting, between Samuel Johnson and Topham Beauclerk, thirty years his junior and quite his equal in the love of argument for

Kuih bahulu. Egg-based and vanilla-flavoured, they have been described as 'Malaysian sponge cakes' and even 'Malaysian muffins'.

argument's sake. Beauclerk stated categorically that 'every wise man who intended to shoot himself took two pistols, that he might be sure of doing it at once'. He went on to give as examples one man who was (by his logic) foolish, and one who was wise:

> Lord —'s cook shot himself with one pistol, and lived ten days in great agony. Mr —, who loved buttered muffins, but durst not eat them because they disagreed with his stomach, resolved to shoot himself; and then he ate three buttered muffins for breakfast, before shooting himself, knowing that he should not be troubled with indigestion; he had two charged pistols.

This story was published in 1791 in Boswell's *Life of Samuel Johnson, Ll. D.* The subject could of course be anybody: Boswell omits the name. His first editor, John Wilson Croker, adds a footnote quoting the news item from the *Gentleman's Magazine* and tentatively inserting the name

Damer. Croker's edition of Boswell (1831) may perhaps be the first occasion on which the subject of this story is named in print (the coroner's report remained in manuscript, and Horace Walpole's letter did not appear in a collected edition until long afterwards). By 1831 there could have been no objection to making the name public. John Damer's father and brothers, his only close relatives, were dead; so was Anne Damer, his widow.

The story told by Topham Beauclerk in 1779 and published by Boswell in 1791 is recognizably the same as the story of 'the man as killed his-self on principle' told by Sam Weller in Dickens's *Pickwick Papers*, published in 1837. Dickens surely borrowed the story from Boswell's *Life of Johnson* but there is no clear sign that he had consulted Croker's edition.

'Wot's the last thing you devoured?' says the doctor. 'Crumpets,' says the patient. 'That's it,' says the doctor. 'I'll send you a box of pills directly, and don't you never take no more o' them,' he says. 'No more o' wot?' says the patient – 'Pills?' 'No; crumpets,' says the doctor. 'Wy?' says the patient, starting up in bed; 'I've eat four crumpets ev'ry night for fifteen year on principle.' 'Vell, then, you'd better leave 'em off on principle,' says the doctor. 'Crumpets is wholesome, Sir,' says the patient. 'Crumpets is not wholesome, Sir,' says the doctor, wery fiercely. 'But they're so cheap,' says the patient, comin' down a little, 'and so wery fillin' at the price.' 'They'd be dear to you at any price; dear if you wos paid to eat 'em,' says the doctor. 'Four crumpets a night,' he says, 'vill do your bisness in six months!' The patient looks him full in the face, and turns it over in his mind for a long time, and at last he says, 'Are you sure of that 'ere, Sir?' 'I'll stake my professional reputation on it,' says the doctor. 'How many crumpets at a sittin' do you think 'ud kill me off at once?' says the patient. 'I don't know,' says the doctor. 'Do you think half a crown's vurth 'ud do it?' says the patient. 'I think it might,' says the doctor. 'Three shillings vurth 'ud be sure to do it, I s'pose?' says the patient. 'Certainly,' says the doctor. 'Wery good,' says the patient; 'good night.' Next mornin' he gets up, has

Muffins, but not the
ones John Damer
died for.

a fire lit, orders in three shillins' vurth o' crumpets, toasts 'em
all, eats 'em all, and blows his brains out.

The subject of Sam Weller's story is anonymous (just as in Boswell's
publication of 1791). The event is timeless, all details have changed and
the breakfast has swollen vastly. Which of these changes took place in
the furnace of Dickens's imagination, and which are to be understood
as a characteristic of the fictional oral tradition through which the story
reached the fictional Sam Weller, the Dickensian critic must decide.

It seems fairly certain (though Croker was hesitant about this) that
the suicide adduced by Topham Beauclerk is that of John Damer, which
had taken place just three years before Beauclerk's conversation with
Johnson. John Damer really did have two pistols, and that was the
only point of Beauclerk's story. If that is agreed, than the story told by
Sam Weller, however transformed, is also that of John Damer.

There is a difficulty, though, at the root of all this. One among the
reports that are close to the event – Topham Beauclerk's story –
mentions the three buttered muffins. Two of the reports that are close
to the event – the coroner's report and Walpole's letter – mention the
four prostitutes. No report combines them. If an event comprises one
significant incident in one source, and a different, equally significant
incident in a second source, the scrupulous historian will hesitate to

write the history of the event by pasting the two sources together: he will, instead, ask why it is so. Did Topham Beauclerk, by taking a couple of slang terms literally, convert a nocturnal debauch to a buttery breakfast? Or, given that breakfast has been so often overlooked in history and memory, did the landlord and the blind fiddler conspire not to mention the muffins?

Freshly baked banana muffins, another variation on the American muffin

Pear and Ginger Muffins

These are, needless to say, American muffins. English muffins, such as those enjoyed by John Damer just before he shot himself, wouldn't be seen dead with pear or ginger.

150 g plain flour
120 g oat bran
90 g soft brown sugar
1 tablespoon baking powder
½ teaspoon salt
½ teaspoon ground cinnamon
180 ml buttermilk or 180 g yogurt
60 ml (4 tablespoons) light vegetable oil
1 egg, beaten
3 small pears, peeled and chopped
75 g crystallized ginger, chopped

Sift the flour into a large bowl with the rest of the dry ingredients. Whisk together the buttermilk or yogurt, the oil and the egg, then add to the flour mixture. Don't over-mix or the muffins will be heavy – a few lumps don't matter. Stir in the pear and ginger. Put into muffin cups and bake for 20 minutes at 200°C.

Crumpets

These quantities will make about 15 crumpets.

200 g strong plain flour
¼ teaspoon salt
¼ teaspoon bicarbonate of soda
1 teaspoon dried yeast
175 ml warm milk
200 ml warm water
oil for frying
butter for serving

Sift the flour, salt and bicarbonate of soda in a large bowl; stir in the yeast. Make a well in the centre, pour in the milk and water and mix to a thick batter. Beat for about 5 minutes with a wooden spoon, then cover and leave to rise in a warm place for about an hour. Beat for another two minutes, and turn into a jug.

Heat a big non-stick frying pan; brush it with a little oil. Use 4 crumpet rings (or 7.5 cm diameter pastry cutters): oil the insides, place them on the frying-pan surface while it is over the heat and let them, too, become hot (about 2 minutes). Pour batter into each ring to about 1 cm thickness. Let them cook for about 6 minutes, till the surface is set. Then remove the metal rings, turn the crumpets over in the pan and cook for just 1 more minute. Put them on a wire rack while continuing with the rest of the batter, oiling the pan and the rings each time.

Then, just before serving, toast the crumpets. Serve hot with the butter.

Eggy Bread

Of the many ways of preparing eggs for breakfast, the three following recipes are among those that denature and homogenize them: the eater can no longer tell that they once possessed a yolk and a white. I'm not complaining; I'm just making an observation.

2 eggs
1 tablespoon milk
salt and pepper

3 or 4 slices bread
butter, lard or (best of all) bacon fat for frying

Beat the egg and milk together, adding a little salt and pepper. Dip the sliced bread in the egg mixture. Melt the butter, lard or bacon fat in a frying pan and fry the eggy bread until golden on both sides. Serve and eat while hot.

Scrambled Eggs

Scrambled eggs is not a single recipe but a school or tradition of recipes. The following simple recipe makes scrambled eggs for one. The quantities can be multiplied, in which case cooking will take just a little longer.

2 eggs
dash of milk
salt and pepper
knob of butter

Beat the eggs with the milk and season with the salt and pepper. Melt 25 g butter in a heavy pan. When it is foaming but not yet brown add the egg mixture. Cut across it with the flat of a spatula so curds start to form; remove from the heat while still slightly liquid, but creamy. Add a little more butter and stir gently.

Butter some hot toast and pour the eggs on top. It tastes better if the toast is cut into ninths like a noughts and crosses board before topping with the eggs (that, at least, is how Mum used to do it).

Those who find scrambled eggs slightly bland can of course mix in a generous blob of tomato ketchup (I've seen it done 50/50). Or they can do something more adventurous as suggested, for example, in the next recipe.

The luxury version: scrambled eggs à la Suisse, served in the pan.

Scrambled Eggs à la Suisse

These quantities will serve 4 to 6. The procedure uses the bain-marie method using two pans, one resting on the other. The lower, water-filled pan is heated; the food in the upper pan is gently and steadily cooked as the water temperature rises. This recipe will take significantly longer than the preceding one (consider this a weekend breakfast recipe) but the effort is repaid.

8 eggs
120 ml single cream
½ teaspoon salt
pinch of cayenne pepper
110 g grated cheese, Gruyère for example
50 g butter or margarine
½ teaspoon chopped chives or parsley

Beat the eggs, cream, salt and cayenne pepper in the upper container until well mixed. Stir in ¾ of the grated cheese and the butter or margarine. Cook over gently boiling water, stirring occasionally, for about 15 minutes, until eggs are set but still creamy. Serve sprinkled with the remainder of the cheese and the chives or parsley.

Biscuits and Gravy

Breakfast at the Joads' in 1930s Oklahoma, as described in John Steinbeck's *The Grapes of Wrath*, consisted quite largely of biscuits and gravy (see pp. 19–20). It is not as outlandish as it sounds to a British reader. Some may even want to try it. For those who do, here are your instructions. First the biscuits, as follows:

225 g self-raising flour
pinch of salt
50 g butter or lard
150 ml milk

Sift the flour and salt together and rub in the butter or lard. Combine the milk with this to make the dough, and knead lightly for half a minute. Roll out to 2 cm thickness (or slightly less); cut into rounds of perhaps 5 cm diameter with a biscuit cutter. Bake for 12 to 15 minutes at 220°C.

Meanwhile, fry your bacon. And meanwhile, make your gravy as follows:

2–3 tablespoons bacon dripping
2 tablespoons flour
140 ml milk
salt and pepper

As if you were making white sauce, make a roux with the dripping and flour, then slowly add the milk. The gravy is ready when it is thick. Serve the bacon and biscuits and pour the gravy over them.

Nasi Goreng

Those who spend time in Malaysia, Singapore or Indonesia are likely to breakfast (perhaps once or twice, perhaps almost daily) on *nasi goreng* or one of its variations. Since this recipe uses ingredients that are mostly already cooked it is very quick to prepare – an important qualification for a breakfast dish. While following the rest of this instruction, don't forget to fry your egg.

2 cloves garlic
3 shallots
2 green chillies
2 tablespoons vegetable oil
2 cooked chicken breasts, shredded or sliced
1 carrot, grated
450 g cold cooked rice
2 tablespoons soy sauce or fish sauce (*kecap manis*)
1 fried egg
3 spring onions, chopped

Finely chop the garlic, shallots and chillies and fry for 2 to 3 minutes in the vegetable oil. Add the chicken and carrot, then the rice. Stir fry and then add the soy sauce. Garnish with a fried egg and the spring onions.

Spanakopita

If the first breakfast in Greece is a cup of coffee, the second is likely to be a hot pastry eaten on the way to work, and *spanakopita* or 'spinach pie' is one of the best. This is unlikely to be made from scratch as a home breakfast – it takes too long – but it could well be bought at the baker's and if necessary reheated at home. This recipe makes about 6.

1 kilo spinach, wilted, chopped and squeezed dry
4 spring onions, sliced
1 small bunch dill, finely chopped
250 g crumbled feta
50 g grated hard cheese such as kefalotyri
2 eggs, beaten
salt and pepper
1 pack filo pastry
olive oil

Mix together the spinach, spring onions, dill, the two cheeses and the eggs. Season this mixture to taste. Taking one sheet of filo at a time, brush with oil and place some of the mix down the length of the sheet. Roll up like a tube, then roll the tube into a spiral. Place the spirals on a baking sheet, tucking the open end underneath. Brush with the oil. Bake for 40 to 50 minutes at 180°C.

Spinach pie
with cheese – the
traditional Greek
spanakopita.

Porridge

Let it be clear: this is oatmeal porridge. Nonetheless a question demands
to be answered: what to begin with. If you begin with real oatmeal, in
the old-fashioned way, you may well prefer to soak it in water overnight.
A bit of advance soaking does no harm to modern, widely marketed
'porridge oats' either. The quantities given below serve 1.

50 g or half a cup of oats
300 ml or 1½ cups of water or milk or half-and-half
pinch of salt

And there, already, the second question – what to cook the oatmeal in –
has been posed. I advise the half-and-half mix of milk and water and I,
for one, will coldly ignore those health-conscious writers who tell me salt
is bad for me. I'd die without salt, and I'm not the only one. Assuming you
have taken the porridge oats option, the method now follows. It takes
about ten minutes. Note that with real oatmeal the cooking process will
take quite a lot longer – about half an hour.

Put the porridge oats, and then the milk and/or water, into a small
saucepan over a fairly gentle heat, stirring occasionally. When the mixture

simmers, turn the heat lower and continue to cook for a few minutes, stirring frequently to ensure it doesn't stick to the saucepan, until it is as thick as you want it.

When using porridge oats the cooking can be done perfectly well in a glass bowl in a microwave; it takes nearly as long but it won't need stirring. I eliminated the microwave (it didn't justify its space, because porridge was the only good thing that ever came out of it) and I nearly always remember to stir the saucepan. Now comes the last question but one: with what to mix the porridge. Ignoring some more health-conscious writers you might well mix in some full cream milk or even cream and you may well add sugar (or honey). Traditionally Scots add not sugar but salt. Less traditionally, some now add fruits, fresh or dried, and nuts, the end result being hot soggy muesli.

The last question is whether to save some of the porridge to eat cold. Fashion has largely answered this: for some reason the old Scottish custom of a porridge drawer in the kitchen, in which the porridge cooled and set, has been widely abandoned.

Devilled Kidneys

'If you think you don't like kidneys, or you're not quite sure,' says Hugh Fearnley-Whittingstall encouragingly in *The River Cottage Meat Book*, 'this is the recipe for you.' Leopold Bloom in Joyce's *Ulysses* (see page 153) was in no such doubt. Fearnley-Whittingstall adds that the dish takes just a few minutes to prepare, which certainly helps to explain its popularity beyond the Joycean community. The River Cottage recipe, showing commendable concern for health, allows the alternatives of 'a little fat or oil (sunflower or olive)' and doesn't tell you to coat the kidneys in flour. Redcurrant jelly is hard to beat but there's no harm in experimentation. The following recipe serves 2.

4 lamb's kidneys, quartered
1 tablespoon flour
cayenne pepper, salt and black pepper
butter (or oil) for frying
2 tablespoons dry reserve sherry
1 tablespoon wine vinegar
1 teaspoon redcurrant jelly
1 tablespoon Worcestershire sauce

1 tablespoon mustard
1 tablespoon double cream

Dredge the kidneys in the flour, ready seasoned with salt and cayenne pepper. Fry them in the butter or oil for about a minute; add the sherry; then the vinegar; then the redcurrant jelly, and stir it in; then the Worcestershire sauce and the mustard. Finally add the cream, and continue to cook in the pan in this sauce for a couple of minutes, probably grinding in some black pepper and perhaps some more cayenne. You will want toast or fried bread, or maybe biscuits (*Grapes of Wrath* style – see 'Biscuits and Gravy' above) to soak up the sauce when you serve.

Huevos Rancheros

A Mexican delicacy that may well be a transatlantic reincarnation of the Middle Eastern *shakshuka*. In its Mexican form it has become an international dish.

If the eggs file for divorce (thus becoming *huevos divorciados* instead of *huevos rancheros*) then make sauces separately for each egg, using a sweet red pepper for one and a green pepper for the other.

1 medium onion, chopped
half a green pepper and half a yellow pepper, chopped
1 clove garlic, crushed

Huevos rancheros. Whether invented in Mexico or not, this is now commonly seen as the traditional Mexican breakfast.

1 can (about 400g) tomatoes
½ teaspoon chilli powder (or more to taste)
½ teaspoon cumin
paprika, salt, pepper
1 tablespoon fresh chopped coriander
4 tortillas
4 fried eggs
tabasco sauce to taste

Sauté the onion and peppers, add the garlic and fry until soft. Add the tomatoes, chilli powder and cumin, season and simmer for 10 minutes until thickened. Sprinkle with the coriander. Serve with soft tortillas and fried eggs.

Refried beans are a frequent addition. Wilder spirits have been known to add cheese or sour cream.

Churros

These, too, might possibly be a reincarnation – of the *youtiao* of southern China.

180 g plain flour
1 teaspoon baking powder
½ teaspoon salt
500 ml water
oil for frying
caster sugar and ground cinnamon for dusting

Sift the flour together with the baking powder and salt. In a saucepan bring the water to boiling point before pouring in the flour, then beating with a wooden spoon until the dough starts to come away from the sides of the pan. Remove from the heat and continue beating until smooth.

Heat plenty of oil in a deep frying pan. When hot, pipe the dough through the large star-shaped nozzle of a pastry bag straight into the pan, to form long strips. Fry, turning once, for a total of 2 to 4 minutes, then drain on kitchen paper.

Serve dusted with sugar and cinnamon, perhaps dipped in thick hot chocolate.

Churros, also known as Spanish doughnuts.

Kedgeree

The origin of kedgeree as a breakfast dish of medieval India, a mixture of rice with beans, is sketched in chapter Three. It was perhaps the British who first took to eating fish with it. Kedgeree in England is still the 'mess of re-cooked fish' with rice that Henry Yule and Andrew Burnell so enticingly described in their nineteenth-century Anglo-Indian dictionary *Hobson-Jobson* – and is all the better for it.

450 g smoked haddock
thick slice of butter
175 g basmati rice
1 tablespoon curry powder
3 hard-boiled eggs
salt and pepper
small bunch of parsley, chopped
handful of sultanas (optional)
chutneys such as mango chutney, brinjal pickle, lime pickle

Poach the haddock in just enough water to cover it, then skin and set aside, reserving the liquid. Melt the butter in a heavy pan and cook the rice and curry powder in it until the grains start to turn translucent. Add nearly double the quantity of water (including the poaching liquid) as rice to the pan, cover tightly and leave on a low heat for 8 minutes. After this time add the fish, breaking it up gently, and two roughly chopped eggs. Season with pepper and a little salt, re-cover and leave for a further 3 to 4 minutes before fluffing the rice with a fork while carefully mixing it with the fish and eggs. Serve on a warm platter garnished with the parsley, the sultanas if you wish, the third egg (quartered) and your choice of pickles.

Paratha

Parathas need not be stuffed, but the paratha recipe below – which is based on Madhur Jaffrey's in *The Essential Madhur Jaffrey* – is followed by a suggested filling, one that suits the context of breakfast because it relies partly on ready-cooked food – boiled potatoes. This makes 8 parathas.

about 9 tablespoons vegetable oil
115 g wholemeal flour
115 g plain flour (and extra for dusting)
175 ml water
½ teaspoon salt

Mix the flours with the salt. Rub 2 tablespoons of the oil into the flour with your fingers, then slowly add the water and form into a soft dough. Knead for 10 minutes, then set aside for half an hour in a bowl, covered with a damp cloth.

Knead again and divide the dough into eight. Working with one piece at a time while keeping the others covered, form into a ball and roll out on a floured surface until you have a 9 cm round.

Add 1 teaspoon of the filling of your choice, then gather up the edges and twist to close firmly over the filling. Turn the ball over and roll out again to 15 cm, dusting with more flour if it sticks. Heat a heavy frying pan over a fairly low heat, adding 1 teaspoon of oil. When it is hot, start frying the paratha. Cook for 2 minutes, then coat the uncooked side with 1 teaspoon of oil and turn it over. There should be some brown spots on the cooked side. Cook the second side for 3 minutes or so, reducing the heat a little if it colours too much: it needs to be cooked through, filling and all. As each paratha is cooked wrap in aluminium foil to keep warm while you cook the rest.

Paratha, a traditional flatbread from northern India, now familiar all over the subcontinent. For breakfast it may be stuffed with potatoes, panir cheese or keema (minced meat curry).

For the Filling

2 medium boiled potatoes
1 small onion, very finely chopped
1 finely chopped green chilli (seeds removed if you wish)
½ teaspoon garam masala
½ teaspoon ground cumin
small piece of ginger, grated
small handful of chopped green coriander

Mash together all the ingredients; use as filling for the parathas as described above.

Elvers

I asked a neighbour for the most exotic breakfast he could remember. The answer was elvers and beer in East Berlin.

Elvers are the young – but not so very young, three years old in fact – of the eel, *Anguilla anguilla*. They have made their way, in concert with the Gulf Stream, from the Sargasso Sea to the lower reaches of European rivers, and up to now they have done so each spring in very large numbers. If in the near future they and the Gulf Stream fail, that'll be that: elvers as a European seasonal delicacy will be no more. If they continue to arrive, most of them will then continue to die on their way upriver, a journey that dams and falling water levels render more difficult year by year. The best an elver fisherman can do for them is to help a good proportion of them on their way while harvesting others. Good elver fishermen do this, and with their collaboration no harm is done by eating a few elvers in season for breakfast.

Clean and rinse the elvers several times in brine. When they are no longer slimy, fry them in bacon fat for about a minute. Transparent when fresh (hence the alternative name 'glass eels'), they will turn white and opaque as they cook. Serve with a glass of beer – or, in the English West Country, cider.

This is the simplest way. There are several alternatives, one of which is to add beaten egg to the pan while the elvers are frying, thus producing an elver omelette. Another is to marinade and flour the elvers before frying: Antony Worrall Thompson has suggested using a marinade of olive oil with lemon juice, a little crumbled dried chilli and a clove of garlic; dipping them briefly in milk; dredging them in flour mixed with cayenne pepper and garlic salt; then frying. Good, but not the Berlin method.

Curried Dog

The most exotic breakfast *I* can remember was minced dog at a village in northern Thailand. To ensure best quality, I was advised, brown dog, not black dog, must be chosen. It was perfectly good (better because I didn't know it was dog until after eating it) but I'm not likely to try it again. For those who prefer not to try it even once I provide a recipe that is just as good, and in all likelihood better, with minced pork.

This serves 4.

2 tablespoons peanut oil (or olive oil)
2 tablespoons mustard seeds
2 teaspoons ground cumin
1 teaspoon ground turmeric
2 teaspoons garam masala
3 cloves garlic, crushed
20 g fresh ginger, grated
2 onions, chopped
800 g minced meat (e.g. pork)
125 ml water
¼ cup fresh coriander, chopped

Heat the oil in a frying pan, then fry the mustard seeds for about 2 minutes, keeping them moving. Next add the cumin, turmeric and garam masala and continue to cook for 2 minutes. Add the garlic, ginger and onion and fry, stirring, until the onion softens. Lastly add the minced meat and fry until it is cooked through. Now add the water and simmer in the frying pan for about 15 minutes. Take off the heat and sprinkle with the coriander before serving.

Serve with sticky rice or, if you can't get sticky rice, just rice.

Hot Cross Buns

Hot cross buns were Samuel Johnson's breakfast on Good Friday (see p. 142), and those hot cross buns were certainly homemade. This modern recipe draws on one by Delia Smith.

50 g and 1 teaspoon caster sugar
150 ml warm water
1 tablespoon dried yeast
450 g plain flour
1 teaspoon salt
1 teaspoon mixed spice (a cinnamon, nutmeg and allspice mixture)
75 g currants
50 g chopped mixed peel
50 ml warm milk
1 egg, beaten
50 g butter, melted

Stir 1 teaspoon of the caster sugar into the warm water; sprinkle in the yeast and leave it until a frothy head forms. Meanwhile sift the flour, salt and mixed spice into a mixing bowl and add the remaining sugar, currants and mixed peel. Make a well in the middle, pour in the yeast mixture and the warm milk, the beaten egg and the melted butter. Mix all to a dough, using a wooden spoon at first and continuing with the hands. Add more milk if needed. On a clean surface knead the dough for about 6 minutes, until it is smooth and elastic. Return it to the bowl, cover it with cling film and leave in a warm place for about an hour to rise. Knead it again to reduce it to its original size.

Divide the mixture into 12 round buns, place them well apart on a greased baking sheet, and with a knife make a deep cross on the top of each. Leave them to rise again, covered, for half and hour or a little less. Meanwhile, heat the oven to 220°C. Bake the buns for about 15 minutes. When they emerge you will want a glaze for them:

2 tablespoons granulated sugar
2 tablespoons water

Melt the sugar and water over low heat. As soon as the buns are baked, brush them with this sticky glaze.

No-bake Nutty Granola Bars

Makes 12 bars (so one can go in each lunchbox if you have twelve children).

180 g rolled oats
150 g chopped walnuts, almonds or a mixture
40 g butter
120 ml liquid honey
45 g dark brown sugar
120 g crunchy peanut butter
75 g raisins

Line a 23-cm square tin with baking parchment. In a hot oven toast the oats together with the nuts, then set aside. Melt the butter with the honey, sugar and peanut butter before adding the oat mix and raisins. Mix well and press firmly into the lined tin. Leave to cool and set completely before cutting into bars.

Orange and Cider Marmalade

No English breakfast, it seems, is complete without marmalade. In its modern form it can be made with any juicy citrus fruits from lime to grapefruit. Seville oranges, which have the bite or bitterness that sweet oranges lack, are probably the best choice and are easily bought in the UK because so many people make marmalade. Thanks to the cider, this recipe (which is based on one given long ago to Yorkshire TV's *Farmhouse Kitchen* series by Doreen Allars) works well even with sweet oranges.

700 g oranges, preferably Seville
juice of 2 lemons
1 litre dry cider
600 ml water
1.4 kilos sugar

Wash the oranges, cut them into halves, squeeze out the juice and the pips. Cut the peel into thin strips. Cut the lemons in half and squeeze them too. Put the orange peel and the orange and lemon juice in a large

Two nutritious granola bars.

pan with the cider and water. Tie the pips in a muslin bag and put this in the pan. Heat to boiling point and then allow to simmer for about 1½ hours or until the peel is soft. Meanwhile warm the sugar in a bowl in the oven at 110°C. Take clean jars and place them in the coolest part of the oven to warm.

Remove the bag of pips from the pan, squeezing the juice out of it, and discard them. Add the warmed sugar, stirring it, without boiling, until it is dissolved. Then bring to the boil and boil rapidly until setting point is reached. To test for setting point put a little of the marmalade on a cold saucer, allow it to cool, then tilt the saucer; if a wrinkled skin is seen as the marmalade begins to run, setting point has been reached; if not, continue to boil and test again.

When the marmalade is at setting point, stop heating and remove the scum with a metal spoon. Allow the marmalade to cool for about half an hour: as it cools it begins to thicken, and this delay ensures that the peel will not rise to the top of the jars. Fill the jars very close to the top. If they are available, put waxed tissue circles on the surface of the marmalade; if not, never mind, but close the pot lids tightly at once while the marmalade is still very hot.

If properly sealed this marmalade will keep for months, or indeed years.

Homemade apricot jam heaped generously on a slice of bread. Some prefer it to marmalade.

SOURCES OF QUOTATIONS

Prologue: *Four Breakfasts*

[Homer] *Odyssey* 16.1–54.

John 21:3–13.

Robert Greene, *Friar Bacon and Friar Bungay*, Act v Scene 1; quoted
from J. Churton Collins, ed., *The Plays and Poems of Robert
Greene* (Oxford, 1905), vol. ii, pp. 72–4.

John Steinbeck, *The Grapes of Wrath* (1939), chapter 8.

1 Breakfast: *Origin, Evolution and Name*

[Hippokrates] *Ancient Medicine* 10. Compare W.H.S. Jones, ed. and
trans., *Hippocrates* (Cambridge, MA, 1923), vol. i, pp. 28–31.

Elmham Ordinance (1526). Quoted from *A Collection of Ordinances
and Regulations for the Government of the Royal Household*
(1790), pp. 137–207.

Samuel Pepys, *Diaries*, 25 May 1660; quoted, here and below, from
Robert Latham, ed., *The Shorter Pepys* (London, 1985).

Gabriel Tschumi, *Royal Chef* (1954); quoted via Claire Clifton and
Colin Spencer, eds, *The Faber Book of Food* (London, 1993).

Liber Niger Domus Regis (*c.* 1475); quoted from *A Collection of
Ordinances and Regulations*, p. 22.

Giraut de Borneil, *Sirventes* 67 ('*Ops m'agra*'), lines 21–2; quoted from
Ruth V. Sharman, ed., *The Cansos and Sirventes of the
Troubadour Giraut de Borneil* (Cambridge, 1989), p. 435.
Authorship uncertain.

Song of the Albigensian Crusade, laisse 139, line 35; quoted from
Henri Gougaud et al., eds, *Chanson de la Croisade Albigeoise*
(Paris, 1989), p. 206: see also Janet Shirley, trans., *The Song of the*

Cathar Wars (Aldershot, 1996).

Giovanni Boccaccio, *Decameron*, day 5, tale 8; the translation quoted is G. H. McWilliam, trans., *The Decameron* (Harmondsworth, 1972), p. 461.

Laurent Joubert, *Erreurs Populaires, et Propos Vulgaires, Touchant la Medecine*, (Paris, 1586), vol. II, p. 206.

'The Merry Adventure of the Pardoner and a Tapster' (*c.* 1400); quoted from F. J. Furnivall and W. G. Stone, eds, *The Tale of Beryn* (London, 1887), pp. 3–4; see also John M. Bowers, ed., *The Canterbury Tales: Fifteenth-century Continuations and Additions* (Kalamazoo, MI, 1992).

Sir Anthony Fitzherbert, *The Book of Husbandry* (1523, 1534), section 149; quoted from W. W. Skeat, ed., *The Book of Husbandry by Master Fitzherbert* (London, 1882), p. 101. Attributed in the OED to John Fitzherbert.

2 Breakfast Through Time

Athenaios, *Deipnosophists* [*Epitome*], 11 b–d. Compare S. Douglas Olson, ed., *Athenaeus: The Learned Banqueters*, (Cambridge, MA, 2006), vol. I, pp. 60–63.

Plutarch, *Table Talk*, 726 c–d. Compare Edwin L. Minar et al., eds, *Plutarch's Moralia* (Cambridge, MA, 1961), vol. IX, pp. 160–63.

Martial, *Epigrams*, 13.31.

Suetonius, *Lives of the Caesars*, 'Vitellius', 13.

Apuleius, *Metamorphoses* (also known as *The Golden Ass*), 1.19.

Giovanni Boccaccio, *Decameron*, day 8, tale 2; day 1, tale 5; day 6, tale 2; quoted from G. H. McWilliam, trans., *The Decameron* (Harmondsworth, 1972), pp. 595, 94–5, 486.

Roland at Saragossa 1194–1201; quoted from Mario Roques, ed., *Roland à Saragosse*, (Paris, 1956), p. 39.

Miguel de Cervantes Saavedra, *El Ingenioso Hidalgo Don Quijote de la Mancha* (1605–1615), part 2, chapter 59; quoted from J. M. Cohen, trans., *The Adventures of Don Quixote* (Harmondsworth, 1959), p. 847.

Almanach des Gourmands [by Grimod de la Reynière], vol. I (1803), pp. 59–62; vol. II (1804), pp. 41–2 and 47–8.

Duff Cooper on Talleyrand in *Wine and Food* (1934); cited via Cyril Ray, *The Gourmet's Companion* (London, 1963).

William Shakespeare, *Henry IV part 1*, Act I Scene 2; Act II Scene 1.

Samuel Pepys, *Diaries*, 6 January, 28 February, 2 May, 30 May and 22 September 1660. See also Robert Latham, ed., *The Shorter Pepys* (London, 1985), p. 144.

George Borrow, *The Bible in Spain* (1843), chapter 50.

'The Voyage of Don Manoel Gonzalez to Great Britain' [1730] in John Pinkerton, *A General Collection of the Best and Most Interesting Voyages and Travels* (London, 1808), vol. II, p. 145.

James Boswell, *The Life of Samuel Johnson, Ll. D.* (1791), year 1737.

Henry Mayhew, *London Labour and the London Poor* (1861), vol. I, p. 60.

Edward Lear, 'Washing My Rose-coloured Flesh'; quoted from Vivien Noakes, ed., *Edward Lear: The Complete Verse and Other Nonsense* (London, 2001), p. 153.

Thomas Babington Macaulay, letter to his sister, 1 June 1831.

Charles Dickens, *Bleak House* (1853), chapter 26.

Edmund Gosse, 'The Poet at the Breakfast Table', from a letter to Austin Dobson (1877); quoted from Evan Charteris, *The Life and Letters of Sir Edmund Gosse* (London, 1931), p. 99.

Mrs Beeton's Book of Household Management (1907 edition), pp. 1720 and 1722 [first published 1861].

George Orwell, 'England your England', in his *The Lion and the Unicorn* (London, 1941).

Jerome K. Jerome, *Three Men in a Boat* (1889).

Eileen White, 'First Things First: The Great British Breakfast', in C. Anne Wilson, ed., *Luncheon, Nuncheon and Other Meals* (Stroud, 1994), p. 1.

Kaori O'Connor, *The English Breakfast* (2006), introduction.

Jane Austen, *Mansfield Park* (1814), chapter 29.

Thomas Love Peacock, *Headlong Hall* (1816), chapters 2 and 7.

Thomas Love Peacock, *Crotchet Castle* (1831), chapter 2.

R. S. Surtees, 'A Hunt Breakfast with Jorrocks', *The New Sporting Magazine*, IV (1832–3), pp. 242–5 (reprinted in *Jorrocks' Jaunts and Jollities*, 1838).

Anthony Trollope, *The Warden* (1855), chapter 8.

Hermann, Fürst von Pückler-Muskau, *Tour in England, Ireland, and France, in the Years 1828 and 1829* (1832), vol. II, p. 57.

Mary Howitt; quoted via Brian Hill, *The Greedy Book* (London, 1966), p. 14.

Edward Spencer Mott, *A Mingled Yarn* (1898) pp. 14–15.

Nancy Mitford, *The Water Beetle* (London, 1962).

Arnold Palmer, *Movable Feasts* (Oxford, 1952).

Establishment of Prince Henry (1610); quoted from *A Collection of Ordinances and Regulations for the Government of the Royal Household* (1790), p. 317.

Samuel Pepys, *Diaries*, 1 January 1661.

Samuel Johnson, *A Journey to the Western Islands of Scotland* (1775), pp. 123–4

Boswell, *The Life of Johnson* at 13 May 1775 and 28 August 1773.

Walter Scott, *Waverley* (1814), chapter 12.

Pückler-Muskau, *Tour in England, Ireland, and France*, vol. I, p. 19.

Thomas Forester, *Norway in 1848 and 1849* (London, 1850), p. 112.

Arthur Conan Doyle, 'The Naval Treaty' (1893); reprinted in his *The Memoirs of Sherlock Holmes* (1894).

Richard Burton, *Goa and the Blue Mountains, or Six Months of Sick Leave* (1851), p. 255.

John Beames, *Memoirs of a Bengal Civilian* (London, 1961), pp. 65 and 81.

Anthony Burgess, *The Enemy in the Blanket* (London, 1958), chapter 6.

Henry Handel Richardson, *The Way Home* (London, 1925), part 2, chapter 2.

Marjorie Kinnan Rawlings, *Cross Creek* (1942); cited via Claire Clifton and Colin Spencer, eds, *The Faber Book of Food* (London, 1993).

Frank Chin, *Donald Duk* (Minneapolis, 1991), p. 147.

Robert Crais, *Voodoo River* (New York, 1995), chapter 6.

Paul Pierce, *Breakfasts and Teas* (1907) pp. 8–9, 37–8.

3 Breakfast Across Space

John Heywood, *Proverbs* (1546), part 2, chapter 9; quoted from J. S. Farmer, ed., *The Proverbs, Epigrams, and Miscellanies of John Heywood* (1906), p. 96.

James Robinson Planché, *Extravaganzas* (London, 1879), vol. V, p. 307.

Cao Xueqin, *The Story of the Stone*, chapter 8; quoted from David Hawkes's translation (Harmondsworth, 1973), vol. I, p. 198.

Charles P. Moritz, 'Travels, Chiefly on Foot, Through Several Parts of England', in John Pinkerton, *A General Collection of the Best and Most Interesting Voyages and Travels* (London, 1808), vol. II, p. 145.

Arnold Palmer, *Movable Feasts* (Oxford, 1952), p. 12.

Mimi Ouei, *The Art of Chinese Cooking*; cited via Cyril Ray,
  The Gourmet's Companion (London, 1963).
Thomas Forester, *Norway in 1848 and 1849* (London, 1850), p. 112.
Thomas Pynchon, *Gravity's Rainbow* (New York, 1973), p. 10.
Peter Goullart, *Princes of the Black Bone* (1959); cited via Claire
  Clifton and Colin Spencer, eds, *The Faber Book of Food* (London,
  1993).
Peter Goullart, *Forgotten Kingdom* (London, 1955), chapter 1.
Edmund Gosse, 'The Poet at the Breakfast Table', from a letter to
  Austin Dobson (1877); quoted from Evan Charteris, *The Life
  and Letters of Sir Edmund Gosse* (London, 1931) p. 99.
William Shakespeare, *King Lear*, Act I Scene 4.
Moritz, 'Travels, Chiefly on Foot', vol. II, p. 144.
François Rabelais, *Gargantua* (1534), chapter 25.
Henry Yule and Andrew Burnell, *Hobson-Jobson* (London, 1903),
  pp. 126, 228, 476.
Edward Spencer Mott, *A Mingled Yarn* (1898), p. 73.
Frances Calderón de la Barca, *Life in Mexico, During a Residence
  of Two Years in That Country* (London, 1843), vol. I, pp. 65, 189,
  239; vol. II, pp. 21–2.
Kingsley Amis, *Lucky Jim* (London, 1954), chapter 17.
Evelyn Waugh, *Labels: A Mediterranean Journal* (1930); quoted via
  Clifton and Spencer, *The Faber Book of Food*.
Spencer Mott, *A Mingled Yarn*, p. 41.
Calderón de la Barca, *Life in Mexico*, vol. I, p. 57.
Hugh Clapperton, *Journal of a Second Expedition into the Interior of
  Africa from the Bight of Benin to Soccatoo* (London, 1829), p. 106.
John Doran, *Table Traits With Something On Them* (London, 1854),
  p. 31.

4 Variables

William Camden, *Remains Concerning Britain*; quoted from the 1674
  edition, p. 400.
James Thurber, 'The Shrike and the Chipmunks', *New Yorker*
  (18 February 1939), reprinted in his *Fables for Our Time*
  (London, 1940).
Orson Scott Card, *Ender's Game* (New York, 1985), chapter 14.
Sir Anthony Fitzherbert, *The Book of Husbandry* (1523, 1534),

section 149; quoted from W. W. Skeat, ed., *The Book of Husbandry by Master Fitzherbert* (London, 1882), p. 101.

'The Voyage of Don Manoel Gonzalez to Great Britain' [1730], in John Pinkerton, *A General Collection of the Best and Most Interesting Voyages and Travels* (London, 1808), vol. II, p. 64.

François Rabelais, *Gargantua* (1534), chapter 21.

Martial, *Epigrams*, 14.223.

Sunan Abū Dāūd, 13.2346–2349.

Maria Edgeworth, *The Absentee* (1812), chapter 5.

Henry Handel Richardson, *The Way Home* (London, 1925), part 2, chapter 2.

Kingsley Amis, *Lucky Jim* (London, 1954), chapter 17.

James Boswell, 'Account of the Escape of the Young Pretender', printed in J. W. Croker's edition of Boswell's *The Life of Samuel Johnson, Ll. D.* (1831).

Apuleius, *Metamorphoses*

Thomas Babington Macaulay, letter to his sister, 1 June 1831.

Fanny Burney, *Evelina* (1778), letters 66 and 47.

Jane Austen, *Mansfield Park* (1814), chapters 28–9.

J.R.R. Tolkien, *The Hobbit* (1937), chapter 2.

J.R.R. Tolkien, *The Fellowship of the Ring*, 2nd edn (1966), pp. 11 and 190. The film adaptation by Peter Jackson (2001) is quoted via the (not necessarily reliable) IMDb or Internet Movie Database.

Guy Beringer in *Hunter's Weekly* (1895); quoted via William Grimes, 'At Brunch, the More Bizarre the Better' in *New York Times* (8 July 1998), Travel, p. 1.

Punch (1 August 1896), p. 2; quoted via *Oxford English Dictionary*, s.v. 'brunch'.

Serlo of Wilton, *Versus de differentiis*, line 108; quoted from Tony Hunt, *Teaching and Learning Latin in Thirteenth-century England: Texts* (Cambridge, 1991), vol. I, pp. 126–31.

Ovid, *Amores*, book 1, poem 13, lines 25–6. Compare Guy Lee, trans., *Ovid: Amores* (Murray, 1968).

Terence, *Eunuchus*, line 732.

Byron, *Don Juan*, canto 2.168–71 (1819).

D. H. Lawrence, *Lady Chatterley's Lover* (1928), chapter 16.

I Kings 4:22.

Midrash Psalms 50:2.

Hermann, Fürst von Pückler-Muskau, *Tour in England, Ireland,*

and France, in the Years 1828 and 1829 (1832), vol. II, p. 64, vol. I,
pp. 19–20.

Edgeworth, *The Absentee*, chapter 14.

Amis, *Lucky Jim*, chapter 6.

Oliver Wendell Holmes, *The Autocrat of the Breakfast Table* (1858),
chapter 10.

Martial, *Epigrams*, 1.87.

Flos medicinae Scholae Salerni, lines 317–21 (other versions are
known as *Regimen sanitatis Salernitanum*); quoted from Salvatore
de Renzi et al., eds, *Collectio Salernitana* (Naples, 1852–9), vol. I,
pp. 445–516.

Humphrey Brooke, *Ygieine or a Conservatory of Health* (1650), p. 107;
cited via Ken Albala, *Eating Right in the Renaissance* (Berkeley,
2002), p. 65.

Edward Hooker Dewey, *The No Breakfast Plan and the Fasting-cure*
(Meadville, PA, 1900), pp. 62–81.

James Boswell, *The Life of Samuel Johnson, Ll. D.* (1791) at 17 April
1778 and 18 April 1783.

'The voyage of Don Manoel Gonzalez to Great Britain', p. 64.

Thomas Hughes, *Tom Brown's Schooldays* (1857).

Gwen Raverat, *Period Piece: A Cambridge Childhood* (London, 1954),
chapter 3.

Henry Mayhew, *London Labour and the London Poor* (1861), vol. I,
p. 29.

Almanach des Gourmands [by Grimod de la Reynière], vol. I (1803),
pp. 61–2.

Isabella Beeton, *The Book of Household Management* (1861), p. 959.

The Breakfast Book (1865); quoted via Eileen White, 'First Things
First: The Great British Breakfast', in C. Anne Wilson, ed.,
Luncheon, Nuncheon and Other Meals (Stroud, 1994).

George Cheyne, *Essay on Health and Long Life* (1724), p. 86; quoted via
Ken Albala, 'Hunting for Breakfast in Medieval and Early Modern
Europe', in *The Meal: Proceedings of the Oxford Symposium on
Food and Cookery 2001* (Totnes, Devon, 2002), pp. 20–30.

John Doran, *Table Traits With Something On Them* (London, 1854),
p. 48.

Diane Ackerman, *A Natural History of the Senses* (1990); quoted via
Claire Clifton and Colin Spencer, eds, *The Faber Book of Food*
(London, 1993).

Saki [H. H. Munro], 'Filboid Studge', in *The Chronicles of Clovis* (1911).

Armistead Maupin, *Tales of the City* (1978).

James Boswell, *The Journal of a Tour to the Hebrides* (1785) at 28 August 1773.

Oliver Wendell Holmes, *The Professor at the Breakfast-table* (1859), chapter 1.

Edward Spencer Mott, *A Mingled Yarn* (1898), p. 41.

James Joyce, *Ulysses* (1922), chapter 2.

John Beames, *Memoirs of a Bengal Civilian* (1961), p. 65.

D. H. Lawrence, *Lady Chatterley's Lover*, chapter 16.

Spencer Mott, *A Mingled Yarn*, pp. 14–15.

Diana Cooper, *The Light of Common Day* (London, 1959).

Pückler-Muskau, *Tour in England, Ireland, and France*, vol. I, p. 45.

George Orwell, 'How the Poor Die' (1946); 'The Spike' (1931); 'A Hanging' (1931).

Charlotte Brontë, *Jane Eyre* (1847), chapter 5.

Geoffrey C. Warren, ed., *The Foods We Eat* (1958)

5 Feeling for Breakfast

James Joyce, *Ulysses* (1922), chapter 2.

Fanny Burney, *Evelina* (1778), letter 17.

G. E. Morrison, *An Australian in China* (London, 1895), p. 143.

Thomas Forester, *Norway in 1848 and 1849* (London, 1850), pp. 110–13.

Breakfast on Pluto, film adaptation (2005) by Patrick McCabe and Neil Jordan, quoted via the (not necessarily reliable) IMDb or Internet Movie Database.

Laurence Sterne, *Tristram Shandy* (1765), vol. VIII, chapter 11.

Robert Latham, *The Diary of Samuel Pepys: Vol. X – Companion* (London, 1983), p. 144.

The Family Book, or Instructions Concerning all the Relations of Life (1835), p. 211.

E. C. Brewer, *Dictionary of Phrase and Fable*, 2nd edn (1871), s.v. 'Disorder'.

A. Bertram Chandler, 'Last day', *Fantastic Worlds* (summer 1953).

Valerius Maximus, *Factorum et dictorum memorabilium libri*, 3.2 ext. 3.

Plutarch, *Spartan Sayings*, 225d.

E. B. Ramsay, *Reminiscences of Scottish Life and Character*, series 2 (Edinburgh, 1861), p. 61.

Thomas Love Peacock, *Crotchet Castle* (1831), chapter 2.

Edward Playter, *Elementary Anatomy, Physiology and Hygiene for the Use of Schools and Families* (1879), p. 120.

M. Tarbox Colbrath, *What to Get for Breakfast* (Boston, 1882), p. 9.

Philip E. Muskett, *The Art of Living in Australia* (London, 1893), p. 57.

Robert Barr, *A Woman Intervenes* (London, 1896), chapter 7.

Henry Handel Richardson, *The Way Home* (London, 1925), part 2, chapter 2.

Henry Handel Richardson, *Ultima Thule* (London, 1929), part 2, chapter 6.

Samuel Johnson, letter to Mrs Thrale (28 June 1783) in G. B. Hill, ed., *Letters of Samuel Johnson, Ll. D.* (Oxford, 1892), vol. II, p. 280.

Sir Walter Scott, *Waverley* (1814), chapter 12.

Jane Austen, *Mansfield Park* (1814), chapter 29.

John Steinbeck, *The Grapes of Wrath* (1939), chapter 8.

Franz Kafka, *Die Verwandlung* [*Metamorphosis*], (1915).

Henry Mayhew, *London Labour and the London Poor* (1861), vol. I, p. 60.

Jerusalem Talmud, Sanhedrin iii, 21c.

Jane Austen, *Northanger Abbey* (1818), chapter 22.

Samuel Pepys, *Diaries*, 1 January 1661.

Thomas Babington Macaulay, letter to his sister, 1 June 1831.

Harriet Beecher Stowe, *Sunny Memories of Foreign Lands* (London, 1854) vol. II.

Henry James, *The Middle Years* (1917), chapters 3 and 1.

Charles Dickens, *Bleak House* (1853), chapter 43.

Thomas Hughes, *Tom Brown's Schooldays* (1857).

[Richard Barham], 'The Knight and the Lady: A Domestic Legend of the Reign of Queen Anne' in *Bentley's Miscellany* (1843), vol. XIII, pp. 304–12; reprinted in *The Ingoldsby Legends* (1879), chapter 49.

Hermann, Fürst von Pückler-Muskau, *Tour in England, Ireland, and France in the Years 1826, 1827, 1828 and 1829* (Philadelphia, 1833), p. 65.

George Borrow, *Wild Wales* (1862), chapter 50.

P. G. Wodehouse, *Thank You, Jeeves* (1934), 'Breakfast-time at the Hall' and subsequent chapters.

Epilogue: *Damer's Muffins*

Journal of Lady Mary Coke (8 February 1767); quoted via C. R. Fay, *Adam Smith and the Scotland of His Day* (Cambridge, 1956), p. 79.

Horace Walpole, Letter to Sir Horace Mann, 20 August 1776 (*Letters*, 1906 edition, no. 1601: vol. VI, p. 368).

Gentleman's Magazine (August 1776).

City of Westminster Coroners: 'Coroners' inquests into suspicious deaths', 1776, pp. 339–43.

James Boswell, *The Life of Samuel Johnson, Ll. D.* (1791) at 13 May 1775 and 28 August 1773.

Charles Dickens, *The Posthumous Papers of the Pickwick Club* (1836–7), chapters 43–4.

Ackerman, Diane, *A Natural History of the Senses* (New York, 1990)

Albala, Ken, *Eating Right in the Renaissance* (Berkeley, 2002)

—, 'Hunting for Breakfast in Medieval and Early Modern Europe',
    in *The Meal: Proceedings of the Oxford Symposium on Food and
    Cookery 2001* (Totnes, Devon, 2002), pp. 20–30

Buck, Carl Darling, *A Dictionary of Selected Synonyms in the Principal
    Indo-European Languages* (Chicago, 1949)

Burnett, J., *Plenty and Want: A Social History of Diet in England from
    1815 to the Present Day* (London, 1979)

Calvo, Manuel, 'Migration et alimentation', *Social Science Information:
    Informations sur les sciences sociales* XXI (1982), pp. 383–446

Clifton, Claire, and Colin Spencer, eds, *The Faber Book of Food*
    (London, 1993)

Cordain, Loren, et al., 'Origins and Evolution of the Western Diet:
    Health Implications for the 21st Century', *American Journal of
    Clinical Nutrition*, LXXXI (2005), pp. 341–54 and at
    www.ajcn.org/content/81/2/341.long

Day, Ivan, 'The Great British Breakfast' in his *Eat, Drink and Be
    Merry: The British at Table, 1600–2000* (London, 2000), pp. 92–6

Doran, John, *Table Traits with Something on Them* (London, 1854)

Douglas, Mary and M. Nicod, 'Taking the Biscuit', *New Society*, XXX
    (1974), pp. 744–7

Farb, Peter and George Armelagos, *Consuming Passions: The
    Anthropology of Eating* (Boston, 1980)

Fieldhouse, Paul, *Food and Nutrition: Customs and Culture*
    (London, 1986)

Grivetti, Louis E., 'America at Breakfast', *Nutrition Today*, XXX/3

(May 1995), pp. 128–34

Hassoun, Jean-Pierre, 'Pratiques alimentaires des Hmong du Laos en France: "manger moderne" dans une structure ancienne', *Ethnologie française*, n.s., XXVI (1996), pp. 151–67

Hill, Brian, *The Greedy Book* (London, 1966)

Khare, R. S., 'The Indian Meal: Aspects of Cultural Economy', in R. S. Khare and M. S. Rao, eds, *Aspects in South Asian Food Systems: Food, Society and Culture* (Durham, NC, 1986), pp. 159–83

Khare, R. S., and M. S. Rao, eds, *Aspects in South Asian Food Systems: Food, Society and Culture* (Durham, NC, 1986)

Latham, Robert, *The Diary of Samuel Pepys. Vol. 10: Companion* (London, 1983)

Lehmann, Gilly, 'Meals and Mealtimes, 1600–1800' in *The Meal: Proceedings of the Oxford Symposium on Food and Cookery 2001* (Totnes, Devon, 2002), pp. 139–54

—, and Mercedes Perez Siscar, 'Food and Drink at the Restoration' in *Petits propos culinaires*, 59 (1998), pp. 15–25

McMillan, Sherrie, 'What Time is Dinner?', *History Magazine* (October/November 2001) and at www.history-magazine.com/dinner2.html

The Meal: Proceedings of the Oxford Symposium on Food and Cookery 2001 (Totnes, Devon, 2002)

Milton, Katharine, 'Hunter-gatherer Diets: A Different Perspective', *American Journal of Clinical Nutrition*, LXXI (2000), pp. 665–7 and at www.ajcn.org/content/71/3/665.long

[Mott], Edward Spencer, *Cakes and Ale* (London, 1913)

Mullan, John, 'Ten of the Best Breakfasts in Literature', *Guardian* (17 April 2010)

Murphy, Christopher P. H., 'Piety and Honor', in R. S. Khare and M. S. Rao, eds, *Aspects in South Asian Food Systems: Food, Society and Culture* (Durham, NC, 1986), pp. 85–119

O'Connor, Kaori, *The English Breakfast: The Biography of a National Meal with Recipes* (London, 2006).

Palmer, Arnold, *Movable Feasts* (London, 1952)

Pereira, Mark A. and others, 'Effect of Breakfast Frequency and Quality on Glycemia and Appetite in Adults and Children', *Journal of Nutrition* (2010)

Pouyat, E., 'Les déjeuners de Paris', *Paris ou le livre des cent-et-un*, XV (Paris, 1834), pp. 269–77

Prakash, Om, *Economy and Food in Ancient India, Part 2: Food* (Delhi, 1987)

Ray, Cyril, ed., *The Gourmet's Companion* (London, 1963)

Waldmann, E. , 'The Ecology of the Nutrition of the Bapedi, Sekhukuniland', in J.R.K. Robson, ed., *Food, Ecology and Culture* (New York, 1980), pp. 47–59

Warren, Geoffrey C., ed., *The Foods We Eat: A Survey of Meals, Their Content and Chronology by Season, Day of the Week, Region, Class and Age* (London, 1958)

White, Eileen, 'First Things First: The Great British Breakfast', in C. Anne Wilson, ed., *Luncheon, Nuncheon and Other Meals* (Stroud, 1994), pp. 1–32

—, 'The Ideal and the Real: Breakfast at the Dawn of the Twentieth Century', in Ivan Day, *Eat, Drink and Be Merry: The British at Table, 1600–2000* (London, 2000), pp. 97–103

Online Resources

'Meal times' at www.foodtimeline.org/foodfaq7.html

'The Early Days of Breakfast Cereal' at www.mrbreakfast.com/article.asp?articleid=13

'James Joyce's Burnt Kidney Breakfast' at biblioklept.org/2011/11/23/james-joyces-burnt-kidney-breakfast-2/

Andrea Hansmeier, *'Kraut, Würste, Bier . . .' – Essen und Trinken in Deutschland. Möglichkeiten und Grenzen von hypermedialen Programmen im fremdkulturellen Verstehensprozeß* Chapter 4 of this dissertation focuses on breakfasts and is worth a glance: http://www.uni-mannheim.de/mateo/verlag/diss/hansmeier/kap-04.html

Megan McKinlay, 'Churchill's Black Dog?' at www.blackdoginstitute.org.au/docs/McKinlay.pdf

ACKNOWLEDGEMENTS

My thanks to Susan Weingarten for Talmudic references, and very special thanks to Rachel, without whose help the recipe section would scarcely exist.

PHOTO ACKNOWLEDGEMENTS

The author and the publishers wish to express their thanks to the below sources of illustrative material and/or permission to reproduce it:

Bundesarchiv: pp. 102 (Bild 135-S-12-08-35/Ernest Schäfer), 169 (Bild 183-R34687), 174 (Plak 003-023-007), 176 (Bild 102-01359A/Georg Pahl); CB and GK: p. 88; Elchavobeer: p. 20; Federal Emergency Management Agency (FEMA), Washington: p. 24 (Marin Nauman); Istockphoto: pp. 6 (Meliha Gojak), 82 (Leah-Anne Thompson), 84 (Terraxplorer), 111 (antb), 191 (JacobVanHouten), 205 (TheCrimsonMonkey); Rex Features: pp. 79, 81; Shutterstock: pp. 91, 107, 160 (Monkey Business Images), 132 (Bernd Juergens), 112 (bonchan), 119 (MSPhotographic), 138 (Joe Gough), 159 (ILYA AKINSHIN), 164, 203 (Glenn Price), 187 (mypokcik), 189 (osov), 196 (Viktor1), 199 (shtukicrew), 209 (Andy Dean Photography), 211 (DUSAN ZIDAR); U.S. Library of Congress, Washington: pp. 26, 66, 83, 99, 115, 126, 170, 183, 184; U.S. National Archives, Washington: pp. 19, 150; O. Vaering: p. 131; Wagaung: p. 105.

INDEX

page numbers in *italic* indicate illustrations; page numbers in **bold** indicate recipes